**New Directions for
Teaching and Learning**

Marilla D. Svinicki
EDITOR-IN-CHIEF

R. Eugene Rice
CONSULTING EDITOR

Supplemental Instruction:
New Visions for Empowering Student Learning

Marion E. Stone
Glen Jacobs
EDITORS

Number 106 • Summer 2006
Jossey-Bass
San Francisco

SUPPLEMENTAL INSTRUCTION: NEW VISIONS FOR EMPOWERING STUDENT LEARNING
Marion E. Stone, Glen Jacobs (eds.)
New Directions for Teaching and Learning, no. 106
Marilla D. Svinicki, Editor-in-Chief
R. Eugene Rice, Consulting Editor

Microfilm copies of issues and articles are available in 16mm and 35mm, as well as microfiche in 105mm, through University Microfims, Inc., 300 North Zeeb Road, Ann Arbor, Michigan 48106-1346.

NEW DIRECTIONS FOR TEACHING AND LEARNING (ISSN 0271-0633, electronic ISSN 1536-0768) is part of The Jossey-Bass Higher and Adult Education Series and is published quarterly by Wiley Subscription Services, Inc., A Wiley Company, at Jossey-Bass, 989 Market Street, San Francisco, California 94103-1741. Periodicals postage paid at San Francisco, California, and at additional mailing offices. POSTMASTER: Send address changes to New Directions for Teaching and Learning, Jossey-Bass, 989 Market Street, San Francisco, California 94103-1741.

New Directions for Teaching and Learning is indexed in College Student Personnel Abstracts, Contents Pages in Education, and Current Index to Journals in Education (ERIC).

SUBSCRIPTIONS cost $80 for individuals and $180 for institutions, agencies, and libraries in the United States. Prices subject to change. See order form at end of book.

EDITORIAL CORRESPONDENCE should be sent to the editor-in-chief, Marilla D. Svinicki, Department of Educational Psychology, University of Texas at Austin, One University Station, D5800, Austin, TX 78712.

www.josseybass.com

CONTENTS

FROM THE SERIES EDITOR

About This Publication. Since 1980, New Directions for Teaching and Learning (NDTL) has brought a unique blend of theory, research, and practice to leaders in postsecondary education. NDTL sourcebooks strive not only for solid substance but also for timeliness, compactness, and accessibility.

The series has four goals: to inform readers about current and future directions in teaching and learning in postsecondary education, to illuminate the context that shapes these new directions, to illustrate these new directions through examples from real settings, and to propose ways in which these new directions can be incorporated into still other settings.

This publication reflects the view that teaching deserves respect as a high form of scholarship. We believe that significant scholarship is conducted not only by researchers who report results of empirical investigations but also by practitioners who share disciplinary reflections about teaching. Contributors to NDTL approach questions of teaching and learning as seriously as they approach substantive questions in their own disciplines, and they deal not only with pedagogical issues but also with the intellectual and social context in which these issues arise. Authors deal on the one hand with theory and research and on the other with practice, and they translate from research and theory to practice and back again.

About This Volume. Over a decade ago, NDTL published an issue introducing Supplemental Instruction, which was beginning to gain a foothold in the academy as a way of helping students succeed in difficult courses. Since that time much has been done to advance what Supplemental Instruction includes and how it is delivered. We are pleased to provide this update to those readers who already know about SI and to introduce new readers to its bases and elaborations.

Marilla D. Svinicki
Editor-in-Chief

MARILLA D. SVINICKI is associate professor of educational psychology at the University of Texas at Austin.

EDITORS' NOTES

Over a decade has passed since the last time the International Center for Supplemental Instruction partnered with Jossey-Bass to publish an issue of *New Directions for Teaching and Learning* on Supplemental Instruction (SI). Much has changed since 1994; the world is a very different place. Yet SI appears to have adapted quite well to the changing needs of students and to the continually evolving state of higher education. In fact, in recent years, we have experienced an unprecedented expansion of SI—both geographically and philosophically—into uncharted horizons. This is a very exciting period of time for this movement, and we are pleased to be able to share some of the developments with you in this publication, *Supplemental Instruction: New Visions for Empowering Student Learning*.

We developed this volume in order to examine the wealth of knowledge we have uncovered over the last three decades, since the inception of SI, and to use this understanding to contemplate how SI can best serve the changing needs of today's students. We further wanted to take this time to seriously reflect on how SI might evolve from this point forward. What are the next logical paths for SI? Where are we heading?

We begin the publication by outlining the current educational climate. In Chapter One, Saundra Yancy McGuire discusses the students we serve today and how they have changed in the thirty-plus years since SI began. She also presents an overview of the recent thinking on how students learn.

The topics of the rest of the volume fit into several larger themes. The first set of chapters provides a solid foundational look at SI for the reader less familiar with the model and its adaptations. These chapters not only present the "nuts and bolts" of the now well-established student support model but offer a great deal of insight from the authors' vast collective experiences from the field. Chapter Two, by Maureen Hurley, Glen Jacobs, and Melinda Gilbert, provides a general overview of the SI model, including the SI philosophy, essential components, program structures, key roles, outcomes, and evaluation. In Chapter Three, Joyce Ship Zaritsky and Andi Toce provide a unique perspective from an urban community college program. Chapter Four, by Sally A. Lipsky, discusses the design and components of a training course for SI leaders, and Chapter Five, by Maureen Hurley, Kay Lutjen Patterson, and Kim Wilcox, examines Video-based Supplemental Instruction (VSI), a variation of the SI model. Even seasoned veterans will find valuable and novel information in these chapters.

The second set of chapters addresses the benefits of SI to leaders, faculty, and administrators—individuals not often mentioned in publications about SI. Historically, the literature has focused predominately on the benefits to

NEW DIRECTIONS FOR TEACHING AND LEARNING, no. 106, Summer 2006 © Wiley Periodicals, Inc.
Published online in Wiley InterScience (www.interscience.wiley.com) • DOI: 10.1002/tl.227

1

students. However, in more recent years, we have become aware that SI can offer many advantages to others as well. In Chapter Six, M. Lisa Stout and Amelia McDaniel offer a broad overview of the benefits attained by SI leaders as a result of their participation in SI leadership activities. In Chapter Seven, Sandra Zerger, Cathy Clark-Unite, and Liesl Smith explain how SI can affect faculty and staff development through informal discussions, workshops, trainings, and coursework, and provide institutional benefits as well.

The third set of chapters focuses on current innovations and exciting future possibilities of SI. In Chapter Eight, Sonny L. Painter, Rebecca Bailey, Melinda Gilbert, and John Prior look at ways to use SI in teaching-learning centers and learning communities, and in other technologically advanced adaptations. In Chapter Nine, Carin Muhr and Deanna C. Martin discuss TeamSI, an ambitious attempt to improve both students' deep understanding of their knowledge in a professional discipline—neuroscience—and their self-development as more mature learners and leaders. In Chapter Ten, Glen Jacobs, Marion E. Stone, and M. Lisa Stout address our vision for the future of SI, including exploring the potential for launching SI into the business sector, expanding our worldwide network, and reaching out to developing countries through the dissemination of the VSI model.

We wish to extend our personal thanks to a great number of people who made this volume possible. This was a collective effort on every level. It not only required extensive effort from our authors across the nation and around the world—but nearly every staff member at our center has become involved in some way as well. Special thanks go to Bonnie Painter for hours of meticulous assistance with editing. Additional editorial gratitude is owed to several of our CAD authors: Dr. Maureen Hurley, Melinda Gilbert, and Amelia McDaniel. We appreciate the assistance of Rachel Hughes in preparing several of the figures used in this manuscript. Again, we wish to thank all of the authors who contributed to this review, and did so enthusiastically and punctually! It was a pleasure working with everyone involved.

We appreciate this opportunity to share our perception of the past and our vision for the future. We believe the prospect for SI is bright, filled with unique possibilities for enhanced learning in a more united populous.

Marion E. Stone
Glen Jacobs
Editors

MARION E. STONE *is associate director and research coordinator of the Center for Academic Development and the International Center for Supplemental Instruction at the University of Missouri-Kansas City.*

GLEN JACOBS *is director of and a certified SI trainer at the Center for Academic Development and the International Center for Supplemental Instruction at the University of Missouri-Kansas City.*

1

This chapter presents information on the transformation of higher education, the learning theories on which the Supplemental Instruction (SI) model is based, and the characteristics of today's student population, and concludes with a look at the benefits and challenges of implementing SI in the twenty-first century.

The Impact of Supplemental Instruction on Teaching Students *How* to Learn

Saundra Yancy McGuire

In the past thirty years, cognitive scientists and educators have gained a vast amount of knowledge about the learning process. During this period, concepts such as active learning, collaborative learning, learning communities, learning styles, and student engagement have emerged as prominent components of a new paradigm in education. The new paradigm is necessary because students today are in many ways very different from their counterparts of three decades ago. They are much more diverse in background, interests, entering skill level, and motivation than were their predecessors.

This chapter examines the changes to higher education over the past thirty years, the learning theories on which the Supplemental Instruction (SI) model is based, today's student population, and some of the issues that SI must address to continue to be effective in teaching students *how* to learn.

Transformation of Higher Education

During the past thirty years there has been a significant change in the landscape of higher education. A larger percentage of high school graduates are

The author gratefully acknowledges the assistance of Christopher Guillory, Ph.D. candidate in the Department of Educational Leadership, Research, and Counseling at Louisiana State University, for his assistance in the preparation of this manuscript.

NEW DIRECTIONS FOR TEACHING AND LEARNING, no. 106, Summer 2006 © Wiley Periodicals, Inc.
Published online in Wiley InterScience (www.interscience.wiley.com) • DOI: 10.1002/tl.228

3

attending college (Hansen, 1998), the diversity of the students has increased significantly, and there are considerably more options for students interested in continuing their education past high school. Online degree programs and national universities, such as the University of Phoenix, have sprung up and blossomed. In addition, there has been a shift in the focus of the institutions themselves.

In the early 1990s, institutions of higher education began to transform themselves from "teacher-centered" to "learner-centered" institutions. The focus shifted from the quality of the teaching to the quality of the learning that is occurring (Barr and Tagg, 1995). The shift is also evident in the way that accrediting agencies are now evaluating institutions. Whereas the focus as recently as the 1980s was on course offerings, faculty credentials, and other institutional characteristics, the focus in the past five years has shifted to student learning outcomes—with the requirement that institutions both identify learning outcomes and demonstrate that students have met them. Colleges and universities can no longer be content simply to offer excellent courses taught by outstanding faculty in a variety of disciplines; they must document that student learning outcomes are being met.

This emphasis on student learning is laudable, but student learning outcomes will not be realized if we do not teach specific learning strategies to those who come to higher education institutions with little or no understanding of the learning process. These students must be taught that performing well in college requires higher-level thinking skills: analysis, synthesis, and evaluation. Though most of these students performed quite well in high school by memorizing and regurgitating information, they will discover quite rapidly that these skills will not produce the same results in college. In order for meaningful, lasting learning to occur, students must understand the learning process and recognize that learning occurs at different levels, as described by Bloom's taxonomy, shown in Figure 1.1.

Although faculty generally assume that students know that memorizing information is not the same as learning for application, analysis, synthesis, or evaluation, this assumption is unwarranted. Formally introducing them to differences in the levels of learning is crucial to developing their understanding of these distinctions.

Furthermore, students must have the motivation to use those strategies. The majority of today's students, however, do not come to college with the motivation to assume responsibility for their own learning and must therefore be provided with experiences that increase motivation for strategic learning. As this introductory chapter and later chapters in this volume will illustrate, SI can play a major role both in this seemingly daunting task of teaching students *how* to learn and in motivating them to *want* to learn. SI is an important mechanism for introducing students to the learning process, engaging them in collaborative learning activities, and providing a collegial environment that increases motivation to engage in learning.

NEW DIRECTIONS FOR TEACHING AND LEARNING • DOI: 10.1002/tl

Figure 1.1. Bloom's Taxonomy

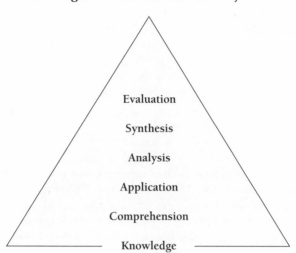

Modern Learning Theories

The SI model has as its theoretical underpinnings the most widely accepted learning theories. These theories emphasize information processing and student-centered learning activities, rather than simply effecting a change in the learner's behavior. A brief overview of the three dominant learning theories that have emerged in the last century will provide readers with a greater understanding of SI's role in shaping student learning.

Behaviorism. B. F. Skinner, the father of behaviorist thought, proposed that learning is represented by a change in behavior, and that this change can be brought about by training the learner to respond appropriately to stimuli. The learning activities suggested by this theory include the drill-and-practice (often referred to as "drill-and-kill") worksheets of the 1960s, and the computer-assisted instruction (CAI) repetitive exercises that were quite prevalent during the 1970s (Rubin, 1996). From the behaviorist vantage point, the learner is viewed as a somewhat passive respondent to the stimuli provided by the instructor, and learning occurs when the correct response is provided the majority of the time—for example, at a rate of 90 percent or higher.

Cognitivism. Jerome Bruner and others proposed that the learning process could not be adequately judged by simply observing behavior, but that it was important to understand what was happening in the mind of the learner (Bates, 1999). Unlike behaviorists, who train the learner to respond in a certain way to certain stimuli, cognitivists view learners as active information processors who are receiving information, processing it, storing it, and retrieving it for use in problem solving and other learning tasks.

NEW DIRECTIONS FOR TEACHING AND LEARNING • DOI: 10.1002/tl

Cognitivists emphasize the need for active, engaged learning, and assert that passive learning is not really learning. In *Reading and Language Arts Worksheets Don't Grow Dendrites,* Marcia Tate presents twenty instructional strategies that engage the brain (Tate, 2005). Some of the strategies she presents are brainstorming and discussion, games, and reciprocal teaching and cooperative learning. These strategies are consistent with the cognitivist view of learning. Employing these strategies and others that she presents will produce a different type of learning than that which results from memorization of lecture notes or textbook material.

Constructivism. Vygotsky and other constructivists view learning as a process during which learners construct their own understanding of a subject by integrating information they are receiving with information they already know (Vygotsky, 1992). Constructivists emphasize the importance of building on the learner's prior knowledge to build new knowledge. The ultimate goal is for the learner to develop his or her own conceptual framework.

Whereas components of all three learning theories are evident in the SI model and activities, it is constructivism that is most closely related to SI activities. In the peer-led, cooperative learning setting of SI sessions, students are required to examine what they know and understand when they come to the session, and are challenged to build new knowledge in collaboration with their peers. The four theories are summarized in Table 1.1.

Numerous research studies have shown SI to be very effective in improving student learning and performance across a number of institutional types (community colleges through medical schools) and educational levels (high school through graduate and professional school) (Bridgham and Scarborough, 1992; Martin, Arendale, and Associates, 1993; Martin, 1980). However, a great challenge to the future effectiveness of SI is enticing a significant number of students in high-risk courses to participate regularly in SI sessions. (Courses are determined to be high-risk when a certain percentage of students taking them repeatedly

Table 1.1. The SI Model: Theoretical Influences

Learning Theory	Learning Process	Learning Activities
Behaviorism	Learner is trained to respond appropriately to stimuli.	Drill and practice; "drill and kill."
Cognitivism	Learner receives, processes, stores, and retrieves information for use in solving a problem.	Engage in active learning.
Constructivism	Learner integrates new information with what she or he already knows.	Integrate "new" information with "old" information to form a conceptual framework.
Supplemental Instruction (SI)	Learner builds new knowledge in collaboration with peers.	Group discussion and problem solving; prediction of test items.

earn D's or F's or withdraw; see Chapter Two for more on this.) When students come to institutions thinking of learning as involving rote memorization and cramming for examinations, they do not understand the need for regular attendance at SI sessions. Many of the characteristics of today's students inhibit their ability to thoroughly understand the importance of attending SI sessions, and therefore undermine their attempts to master college-level course material.

Precollege Learning Habits of Today's Student Population

Most students enter college without knowing how to learn or how to study, and they therefore have difficulty succeeding in courses that require critical thinking. The reasons for their lack of knowledge about how to learn can often be traced to their high school experiences.

Discussions with numerous Louisiana State University (LSU) students about their experiences in high school often reveal that the emphasis was on memorization of information and the examinations involved simply regurgitating the information that they had memorized. Past discussions with students at several other institutions in New York, Tennessee, and Alabama revealed experiences quite similar to those of the LSU students. After their successful academic experience in high school, when these students take university courses they are confident that they can begin studying one or two nights before the test, memorize facts and formulas, and do well on the examinations. They get a rude awakening when this is not the case.

In addition to students knowing little about the learning process, other factors hamper their ability to learn. One of the most important factors is their lack of awareness of the need to spend time studying outside of class. The Higher Education Research Institute (HERI) reported that in 2003 66 percent of entering first-year students at a large Western university spent fewer than six hours per week doing homework in their senior year of high school. Yet 48 percent of these students reported that they graduated from high school with an A average! Furthermore, 70 percent of them felt that their academic ability was above average, or in the upper 10 percent of people their age (Sax, Hurtado, Lindholm, Korn, and Mahoney, 2005). Given such precollege experiences, it is important for today's students to be taught *how* to learn and provided with specific learning tools for success in college-level learning tasks. Supplemental Instruction provides the perfect environment in which to introduce students to the tools they need for success.

SI: Teaching Students *How* to Learn

Cognitive psychologists make a distinction between rote learning and meaningful learning (Ausubel, Novak, and Hanesian, 1978). Rote learning is verbatim memorization of information, and it is not necessarily accompanied by any understanding of the material. Students are unable to explain information that is learned by rote, and they are not able to paraphrase the information in their own words. Meaningful learning, in contrast, is learning that is tied to previous knowledge; students understand the material well enough to manipulate, paraphrase, and apply it to novel situations. Most learning is neither completely rote nor entirely meaningful, and can be placed on a rote–meaningful learning continuum (Ausubel, 1968). Students in SI sessions work collaboratively to understand the course concepts, brainstorm ideas, and engage in discussions of how the concepts relate to each other. Students participating in SI sessions are involved in paraphrasing the course information, using it in different contexts, and even writing potential examination questions. These activities facilitate their greater conceptual understanding, and their success on problem-solving tasks and examinations increases substantially. SI programs at a variety of types of institutions have increased graduation rates, increased the level of confidence of SI participants, and created a welcoming climate for all students—especially minority and women students who may otherwise feel somewhat isolated (Barlow and Villarejo, 2004).

Institutions implementing Supplemental Instruction report that the program benefits all segments of the university population (Arendale, 1997). Participating students report that the SI sessions allow them to view the course material from a different perspective, and that the SI leaders engage them in activities that make learning fun and motivate them to excel. In this engaging, inviting environment, most students shift their learning paradigm from simply memorizing information to perform well on a test or a quiz to learning the material for conceptual understanding. This results in an increase in critical thinking, problem-solving skills, test performance, and grades.

The SI leaders—who are students themselves—also benefit because their own learning improves when they structure learning experiences for the students they are guiding. SI leaders also develop leadership skills, learn how to influence group dynamics, and learn strategies for motivating others to excel. Graduate and professional school admissions committees often find SI leaders particularly attractive candidates for admission because they understand the learning process and are most likely to excel in the graduate or professional school environment.

Faculty members who teach courses in which SI is offered often report that SI allows them to be more in touch with their students' needs. Meetings with their SI leaders provide information on student understanding, problems, and potential trouble spots. This information was not as accessible prior to having SI in their courses.

Future Challenges

Supplemental Instruction has had a substantial impact in a wide variety of institutions. However, significant challenges must be overcome if SI is to meet the needs of twenty-first-century students. Three of the biggest challenges are described here. Subsequent chapters will suggest strategies for addressing them.

Increasing Participation in SI Sessions. Regular attendance at SI sessions has been shown to increase student performance, often quite dramatically (Arendale, 1997). However, many students are reluctant to attend the sessions on a regular basis, opting to attend only before an examination or a quiz. Students can be motivated to attend regularly when the SI leader consistently uses activities that engage students and teach them new strategies for learning, rather than simply reviewing the course content and solving problems. SI leaders who use games and other interactive activities generally get more consistent attendance at their sessions.

Increasing Faculty Buy-In for the SI Program. Because SI is targeted at high-risk, high-enrollment courses, and not simply provided based on instructor request, some faculty do not strongly encourage their students to attend SI sessions regularly. When course instructors enthusiastically embrace SI and vigorously promote it during their lectures, regular attendance at SI sessions is higher than in courses in which this is not the case. It is therefore important for institutions to help faculty members understand the relationship between SI and student learning, and to disseminate information on how the SI program benefits the institution, the students, and the faculty.

Making SI Attractive to the Net Generation. Effective SI sessions involve extensive discussions among the students in the group, with the SI leader serving as a facilitator. However, many of today's students appear to be much more interested in interacting with their computers (e-mailing or gaming), using their cell phones (talking or text-messaging), or playing games on their Xboxes than in interacting with one another to learn course content. If SI is to reach these students, new strategies may need to be used. For example, when leaders e-mail SI participants the discussion topics for upcoming SI sessions, consistency in attendance increases.

Conclusion

This chapter presented information on the current transformation of higher education, the evolution in our understanding of the learning process, characteristics of many of today's students, and some of the benefits and challenges facing Supplemental Instruction as it seeks to continue to increase student learning. The chapters that follow will develop these topics further and present an in-depth look at the historical development of SI, its successes over its thirty-two-year history, its effectiveness with a wide range of students in a variety of settings, and the new directions in which it is moving.

The prognosis for SI is excellent, because it has proven its effectiveness in helping higher education institutions achieve their most important objective: producing graduates who have achieved the student learning outcomes necessary for success in their courses, in their careers, and in making a significant contribution to the global society.

References

Arendale, D. R. "Understanding the Supplemental Instruction (SI) Model," 1997. http://www.tc.umn.edu/~arendoll/Sioverview94.pdf. Accessed Aug. 21, 2005.

Ausubel, D. P. *Educational Psychology: A Cognitive View.* Austin, Tex.: Holt, Reinhart and Winston, 1968.

Ausubel, D. P., Novak, J., and Hanesian, H. *Psychology: A Cognitive View.* Austin, Tex.: Holt, Rinehart and Winston, 1978.

Barlow, A. E., and Villarejo, M. "Making a Difference for Minorities: Evaluation of an Educational Enrichment Program." *Journal of Research in Science Teaching,* 2004, *41*(9), 861–881.

Barr, R. B., and Tagg, J. "From Teaching to Learning: A New Paradigm for Undergraduate Education." *Change,* 1995, *27*(6), 13–25.

Bates, T. A. *"The Cognitivist Epistemology and Its Implications for Instructional Design."* Unpublished paper, George Mason University, March 8, 1999. http://chd.gmu.edu/ immersion/knowledgebase/strategies/cognitivism/cognitivism.htm. Accessed Aug. 18, 2005.

Bridgham, R. G., and Scarborough, S. "Effects of Supplemental Instruction in Selected Medical School Science Courses." *Academic Medicine RIME Supplement,* 1992, *67*(10), 569–571.

Hansen, E. J. "Essential Demographics of Today's College Students." *AAHE Bulletin,* Nov. 1998, *51*(3), 3–5.

Martin, D. C. "Learning Centers in Professional Schools." In K. V. Lauridsen (ed.), *Examining the Scope of Learning Centers.* New Directions for College Learning Assistance, no. 1. San Francisco: Jossey-Bass, 1980, 69–79.

Martin, D. C., Arendale, D., and Associates. *Supplemental Instruction: Improving First-Year Student Success in High-Risk Courses.* Columbia: National Resource Center for the Freshman Year Experience and Students in Transition, University of South Carolina, 1993.

Rubin, A. "Educational Technology: Support for Inquiry-Based Learning." *Infusion and School Change.* Cambridge, Mass.: TERC, 1996, 34–71. http://www.heid-dso.eu.dodea. edu/HMSP/pages/publications.htm. Accessed May 25, 2006.

Sax, L. J., Hurtado, S., Lindholm, J. A., Korn, W. S., and Mahoney, K. M. *The American Freshman: National Norms for Fall 2004.* Los Angeles: Higher Education Research Institute, UCLA, 2005.

Tate, M. L. *Reading and Language Arts Worksheets Don't Grow Dendrites: 20 Literacy Strategies That Engage the Brain.* Thousand Oaks, Calif.: Corwin Press, 2005.

Vygotsky, L. S. *Educational Psychology.* St. Lucie, Fla.: CRC Press, 1992.

SAUNDRA YANCY MCGUIRE is director of the Center for Academic Success and adjunct professor of chemistry at Louisiana State University, Baton Rouge.

2

A general overview of the SI model is provided, including the SI philosophy, essential components of the program, program structures, key roles, outcomes, and evaluation. A review of what we have learned about the importance of planning SI sessions, providing ongoing training for leaders, conducting regular SI program assessments, and implementing effective and essential learning strategies is also provided.

The Basic SI Model

Maureen Hurley, Glen Jacobs, Melinda Gilbert

Supplemental Instruction (SI) was developed by Dr. Deanna Martin in 1973 at the University of Missouri at Kansas City (UMKC) to increase the performance and retention of students in high-risk classes. SI is an academic support program that provides regularly scheduled, out-of-class, peer-facilitated sessions that are open to all students in the course. The students attend the sessions on a voluntary basis. SI leaders—the facilitators—are students who have demonstrated competence in this or a comparable course and have taken part in an intensive two-day training session. The SI leaders attend all class sessions, take notes, read all assigned material, and conduct three or more fifty-minute SI sessions each week. They guide students in learning appropriate study strategies, such as note taking, graphic organization, questioning techniques, vocabulary acquisition, and test preparation, while also reviewing content material. The program also has an SI supervisor. The SI supervisor identifies the targeted courses, is responsible for gaining faculty support, selects and trains SI leaders, monitors SI sessions for quality, and evaluates the program (University of Missouri-Kansas City, 2005).

Philosophy of the Model

The philosophy behind the SI model is based on a collection of learning theories. SI borrows several behavioral learning principles from Skinner (Epstein, 1982), Bandura (1977), Ausubel (1967), and Herbart (1895). The first behavioral learning principle is that behavior is based on positive reinforcement. When students learn a new study strategy that helps them do

NEW DIRECTIONS FOR TEACHING AND LEARNING, no. 106, Summer 2006 © Wiley Periodicals, Inc.
Published online in Wiley InterScience (www.interscience.wiley.com) • DOI: 10.1002/tl.229

well on a test, they will continue to use that strategy. Second, it is important to break down complex tasks into their component parts. When a student does not understand a complex task the SI leader teaches the student how to break it down into smaller parts. Working on a task piece by piece can be less overwhelming and can help a student better understand a concept as he or she goes along. Third, it is important to emphasize cause-and-effect relationships: good study strategies result in good performances. Finally, modeling is important. SI leaders need to model good study strategies for their students.

SI also borrows several cognitive developmental principles from Bruner (1968), Piaget (1932/1973), and Flower and Hayes (1981). First, cognitive structures develop little by little as learning is built through organization and assimilation of new information and experiences. If the SI leader can help students learn how to organize and integrate new information and experiences, then the students will be able to absorb and actually store the information for future retrieval. Second, learners think differently about a concept as they assimilate knowledge. SI leaders help students learn how to think critically about a concept. Third, prior knowledge is used while learning new knowledge. SI leaders help students learn how to relate their prior knowledge to new concepts for better understanding and absorption of information. Finally, cognitive development is stimulated when conflict arises during social interaction. SI leaders encourage students to discuss topics with peers outside of the classroom. When students find that there is a conflict in their information, resolving the conflict causes them to expand their cognitive development.

SI also borrows some social interdependence principles from Geertz (1983), Vygotsky (1986), Bakhtin (1993), Doyle (1983), and Erickson (1982). First, learners actively build knowledge. Students have to take responsibility for their own learning by voluntarily attending SI sessions. Second, it is important to work together cooperatively and interdependently. Students in SI learn to work together to reach common goals. When students work together, everyone's individual knowledge contributes to the task at hand and the students benefit from everyone in the group. Third, knowledge is more thorough when it is produced, not simply distributed. Thus, SI leaders do not lecture the students; instead, they guide students in different study strategies that they can employ on their own. Fourth, knowledge and understanding are constructed in dialogue with others and facts are "true" in that social situation. As mentioned earlier, the students learn from each other. Fifth, learners are able to do in group effort today what they will be able to do autonomously tomorrow. The knowledge students gain in SI can be used in other classes and in different settings in the future.

Finally, SI borrows several interpretive-critical principles from Freire (1988), Apple (1988), and Kozol (1995). First, learners take control of their own learning processes when empowered by good pedagogy, and second, education's goal should be liberation rather than domination. Therefore, SI leaders work to get students to a point where they do not have to rely on their professors for answers. Third, a motivation for educational programs should be to overcome the learner's "culture of silence." A student who does not understand a concept may stay quiet because he is afraid he is the only one who does not understand. SI works to help students break their silence and realize that if they are struggling, then others may also be struggling.

Why and How It Works

SI works because SI sessions are proactive and participatory rather than reactive and passive. SI strives to break what is called the *dependency cycle* or *learned helplessness*. The dependency cycle is a pattern of learned behavior that allows students to remain dependent on an authority figure (the instructor or tutor) for learning. Relying too heavily on repetition, drill, and memorization encourages this dependency. These techniques cause students to fall back into a mode of memorizing isolated facts that is time-consuming and ineffective. Students with sophisticated learning strategies that allow them to convert information into meaningful knowledge will learn with this format; however, students without this sophistication, especially those new to a discipline, will have problems. When these students have problems, they will ask questions, which may lead to their professor telling them the same information again, usually more slowly the second or third time. Repeating the same information more slowly does not correct the problem. The students' failure in one situation may lead them to believe that they cannot learn new complicated information at all. SI works to help students use new learning strategies so they are less dependent on being told information. It enjoys a nonremedial image while offering academic support to all students enrolled in historically difficult courses (University of Missouri–Kansas City, 2005).

SI also works because, besides allowing students to get higher grades and gain effective learning skills, it provides them with peer collaborative learning experiences that promote assimilation into campus culture. SI makes efficient use of study time and provides an opportunity for students to develop relationships with other students and staff, an important factor in retention (University of Missouri–Kansas City, 2005).

Program Structure

There are a number of important decisions to be considered when organizing and maintaining an SI program.

Key People and Roles. There are four key participants in the SI program: the SI leader, the SI supervisor, the student, and the faculty member. Each person plays a key role. The SI leader attends training before classes start, attends the targeted class, takes notes, does homework, and reads all assigned materials. Leaders conduct at least three to five SI sessions each week, choose and employ appropriate session strategies, support faculty, meet with their SI supervisor regularly, and assist their SI supervisor in training other SI leaders (University of Missouri–Kansas City, 2005).

NEW DIRECTIONS FOR TEACHING AND LEARNING • DOI: 10.1002/tl

The SI supervisor assists SI leaders in doing their job. Supervisors provide on-site supervision of the SI program, assist SI leaders with attendance, surveys, scheduling, and faculty relations, and promote the program. SI supervisors also identify weaknesses or problems in the current SI program and solve or make recommendations for their solution (University of Missouri-Kansas City, 2005).

Students voluntarily attend SI sessions for targeted classes and participate in sessions as much as wanted or needed. Faculty make grades from exams available to the SI supervisors to help them determine whether students coming to SI are performing at a higher level than those students who do not. Faculty allow SI leaders to attend class, give them a few minutes at the beginning of class to make announcements about the program, meet with SI leaders on a regular basis during office hours, and share reactions to the SI program (University of Missouri-Kansas City, 2005).

How Classes Are Chosen. SI targets classes that consistently demonstrate 30 percent or higher rates of D's, F's, and withdrawals (DFW's). These classes must also have the instructor's support and be large enough to adequately support SI. The instructor is usually demanding but fair, and SI is assigned to a course because of what is being taught, not because of the manner in which it is being taught. SI does not focus on the student or the professor; it focuses on the difficult course material (University of Missouri-Kansas City, 2005).

Marketing SI. When SI sessions are marketed it ensures that students are constantly reminded of them. There are several ways that SI can be marketed. SI leaders can announce the program during the first class of the semester. This is a good time for an awareness video to be shown that explains and promotes SI. SI bookmarks and stickers can be made and handed out to the students. SI leaders can put information up on an overhead projection before class begins so that students can see it as they walk in. Such an overhead might include an exam score analysis chart showing SI versus non-SI mean grades and advertise concepts that will be covered in the following weeks' sessions as well as note all of the session times, days, and locations. SI leaders can also write the daily SI times and locations on the board during each class (University of Missouri-Kansas City, 2004).

It is also helpful to promote the SI program through academic advising, new student orientation programs, and other means before the academic term begins.

Outcomes of SI. Studies show the benefit of attending SI sessions. SI is proven to increase mean final course grades for students at all ability levels, regardless of prior achievement. A study showing the grades of students from the fall of 1997 to the fall of 2003 showed a significant difference between those who attended SI sessions and those who did not. Attendees had lower percentages of DFW's than those who did not attend. The skills learned for the class that provides SI can also be carried over to other classes (University of Missouri-Kansas City, 2005).

Furthermore, students are not the only ones who benefit from the program. SI leaders benefit by learning material better for their own discipline, learning effective study skills, and learning how to talk about what they know. They also benefit by gaining leadership skills that are positive additions to a resume. Administrators benefit by the increased retention rates produced by the program. And finally, faculty benefit by gaining more time for research since students stop by their office less often because they no longer see faculty as their main source of information (University of Missouri-Kansas City, 2005).

Program Evaluation and Reporting. It is important for SI to be evaluated regularly. The evaluation should be completed at the end of each term after final exams and final grades have been determined. The SI program is evaluated each academic term in order to continuously improve the overall quality of the program. Information about its strengths and weaknesses is gathered to inform college administrators about its overall impact. The program is evaluated by assessing institutional outcome measures such as final course grades, course withdrawal rates, institutional dropout rates, and institutional graduation rates (University of Missouri-Kansas City, 2005).

In addition to revealing the program's strengths and weaknesses and assessing its impact, evaluations help faculty and administrators know how many students the program serves and whether or not students say it is beneficial to them. They also keep the program on the faculty's and administrators' minds. Assessment is important too because it can have a direct link to funding (University of Missouri-Kansas City, 2005).

What We Have Learned: What Worked? What Did Not Work?

We have learned a number of things in our thirty-plus years of providing SI on our own campus as well as from feedback in the field. Lessons learned are in several key areas: (1) the roles of the faculty, supervisor, and leader; (2) session planning; (3) the importance and structure of ongoing training; (4) SI program assessment; and (5) effective and essential learning strategies. Some of these topics were already touched on but will now be discussed in greater detail.

Roles of the Faculty, Supervisor, and Leader. The faculty's role in the SI process has become more and more critical as we look at a team approach to producing the most positive outcomes for participants. Faculty must be supportive of the SI model and understand how the peer-led sessions can help students learn more effectively. They can help coach the leaders in the course content that is most critical for students to understand. When they are available to meet weekly with the leaders, they can help guide the structure of the SI sessions. This also allows them to receive feedback on what is particularly challenging for the students.

Faculty must also visit with the SI supervisor before the term begins to discuss what their role entails. Their lectures cover a good deal of content, but often they do not have time to help students grapple with the nuances of the key elements and important concepts. When faculty are enthusiastic about SI and encourage their students to take advantage of it, they play an important role in motivating them to participate in the sessions. Faculty on our campus and at other institutions say that telling students that SI is a continuation of the class results in greater SI attendance. If leaders are having difficulties with attendance they can ask the professor to share the benefits of SI with the students. It is critical that faculty do not say that SI is for students who are struggling, because once they perceive it as remedial, they will not come to sessions.

We also ask faculty to send the first exam grades to the SI supervisor. This way the data can be analyzed and the mean grade for SI and non-SI participants can be calculated. This can provide a strong incentive for students, who learn that SI participants do better than their nonparticipating counterparts.

The supervisor's responsibilities are quite time-intensive. Supervisors need to interact with administrators to show the value of the program in terms of numbers of students served, cost-effectiveness, course completion, reenrollment and graduation rates, higher course grades, and lower DFW rates. National data are available on studies that show outcomes supporting these elements. Administrators are aware of the cost of recruiting new students versus retaining current ones. Because SI is a group learning model, more students are served in SI sessions than in individual tutoring sessions.

After getting the administrators onboard, it is the supervisor's responsibility to contact deans, department chairs, and individual faculty to discuss the value of attaching SI to selected courses. Supervisors need to look for faculty who are open and receptive to interventions that will help their students learn more effectively.

In starting a program, it is essential to select senior faculty who are well respected by their peers and well liked by students. The supervisor can ask them to recommend a few students who have taken their course and would be good leaders. Next, the supervisor interviews prospective leaders and makes a selection, choosing students who are likely to have a good rapport with program participants and have the time to carry out the duties.

The supervisor and other staff are responsible for booking rooms, producing surveys, organizing training, securing funds for salaries and other expenses, conducting evaluations, keeping in touch with faculty, assisting leaders with planning, observing and debriefing SI sessions, and producing reports. Sufficient release time for supervisors is critical for the quality and success of the program.

Finally, leaders too are essential members of the SI team. Their time commitment is considerable; it includes attending classes, planning sessions, conducting sessions, and meeting with faculty and supervisors. Their training before the term and during the semester should focus on effective learning strategies for their course. They need to set up their sessions in such a way that the students are actively engaged with the material, work with one another, and take away a clear understanding of the content. It is important that leaders be open to suggestions and focus on their students' needs. They do not "re-lecture" but instead provide activities that allow students to think critically, teach one another the material, and learn effective strategies that work for deeper understanding and test preparation. They must provide a dynamic session that will capture the students' attention and make them feel this was a worthwhile use of their time.

Planning the SI Session. There should be a well thought-out written plan for each session. Planning sheets should be used, and must contain session objectives, content to be covered, and processes to be used. Leaders work with both the supervisor and the faculty member to assist them in creating their session plan. The plan is based on the key concepts that were covered in the weekly classes. The objective should state clearly what needs to be accomplished in the session based on those critical elements. Estimated time for each activity should be listed so that the leaders can use the planning sheet as a guide to help stay on task.

Each session should begin by setting the agenda, go on to provide group work that employs one or two learning strategies, and finally provide a closing activity. During the session the leaders need to briefly describe the content to be covered and the learning strategies to be used to accomplish the objectives. It is important for students to feel that their voice is heard and that they have learned something valuable, and it is important for them to be comfortable enough to ask questions and work with other students. Leaders can also be available during office hours to meet with students individually.

As noted earlier, the first day of class is a good time for leaders to talk with the students about SI. Their presentation should be planned and delivered in a way that motivates students to attend. By being present in class each day and taking notes, the leaders can show their interest and involvement in the course. They need to be approachable, talk with students, and encourage them to participate in SI.

Ongoing Training for Leaders. We have found that as important as initial training for leaders is, holding regularly scheduled training meetings throughout the term is even more essential. The focus of these sessions is on both the process and the methodology most closely aligned to course content (University of Missouri-Kansas City, 2005). The International Center for SI recommends that supervisors hold biweekly meetings with leaders to give them regular feedback that can shape their continual session planning. The leaders share their concerns about how their sessions are going and the group, with the supervisor's guidance, problem-solve and determine how the difficult concepts from the lectures can best be approached.

Some training meetings can be led by the leaders. We recommend that leaders in similar content areas design a session plan and present it to the larger group for critique and discussion. Leaders can share the specifics of a plan they used and tell the group what worked well and what did not.

New leaders may feel particularly insecure or lost at the beginning of the term. Veteran leaders can give them valuable advice on how they planned and conducted sessions, what learning strategies worked especially well for them, and how they dealt with difficult issues that arose during the sessions.

Just as the SI model is based on the tenets of collaborative learning, the ongoing training meetings should employ those same kinds of strategies. Some activities can be done with partners or in small or large group discussions. It is always important to allow for report-back from the groups so that the leaders have a chance to explain what they did and how they processed a learning strategy. We have found that without these frequent meetings, leaders may revert to re-lecturing, answering their students' questions, or relying on the same strategies in every session. This can have a negative impact both on the learning that takes place and on attendance.

SI Program Assessment. As already noted, after the first exam faculty are asked for a list of student grades so that they can compare results of SI and non-SI participants. The mean grade of SI attendees should generally be in the range of one-half to a full letter grade higher than non-SI attendees. Having the leader share this information with the class can motivate all students to attend SI sessions.

Next, an evaluation should be completed at the end of the term after final grades are posted. This assessment is needed to compare final course grades and the percentage of DFW's among SI and non-SI attendees. These outcomes help determine the success of the program and give administrators a reason to continue financing it (University of Missouri-Kansas City, 2005).

The program assessment should measure both learning and retention. Lowering the rate of DFW's results in a higher percentage of students completing the course. Studies at UMKC have shown that it also contributes to higher reenrollment and graduation rates.

Administrators want to know the overall success of the program in terms of number of students served, academic progress of students, and cost-effectiveness. Faculty are interested in how students did in their course, who attended SI, and how satisfied students are with the program. It is critical to regularly send reports to faculty and administrators that contain data outcomes as well as narratives on program results. These reports remind them that the program is serving a number of students and contributing to their academic success.

Effective and Essential Learning Strategies. Learning strategies are at the core of SI. In developing SI, Dr. Deanna Martin based the model on the results of leading research. She placed it in the conceptual framework of Piaget's model of cognitive development (Blanc, DeBuhr, and Martin, 1983). Martin's theory considered that many university students arrive with a deficiency in abstract reasoning and the critical thinking skills they need to process information from a lecture. These students may also be unable to read effectively and comprehend key concepts in a textbook (Hurley, 2000). Martin also believed in constructivism, the idea that learning happens best when students construct their own knowledge. SI includes the active engagement of students in the learning process. This is achieved by following specific processing guidelines.

Students who study together learn more by teaching each other (Johnson, Maruyuama, Johnson, Nelson, and Skon, 1981). In the SI sessions it is important for the leader to employ proven learning strategies that allow students to work together (University of Missouri-Kansas City, 2004). It is important to vary the strategies so that students do not become bored. Some techniques are applicable to learning content in any course; other strategies work more effectively in problem-based classes, such as science and math, or in information-based classes, such as history or philosophy.

"Redirecting questions" is a strategy that is central to all types of SI sessions. The goal of this process is to provide a structure in which students interact with one another rather than direct all of their comments and questions to the leader. This may sound like a simple technique, but it is surprisingly difficult for some leaders to master. It is based on the idea that we learn more effectively if we explain something to someone else (Riley, 1981). It is counterintuitive for leaders not to answer a question asked by a student when they are knowledgeable about that content. Therefore, the SI supervisor needs to provide leaders opportunities to practice this strategy during the training meetings. It is helpful if the supervisor models the process and then has the leaders practice the redirecting in pairs, followed by demonstrations for the large group. Examples of this technique can be found in the *Supplemental Instruction Leader Resource Manual* (University of Missouri-Kansas City, 2004).

Using "wait time" is another essential strategy. Wait time is the time that elapses between an SI leader question and a student response (University of Missouri-Kansas City, 2004). It is important to distinguish between the wait time that occurs after the leader asks a question and the wait time that occurs after a student first responds. Wait time is the key to conducting any SI session. The literature on learning suggests that there is a correlation between the level and depth of student responses and the use of at least three seconds of wait time before the person asking the question says anything else (Rowe, 1974). Students need time to think critically and formulate a meaningful answer.

The second wait time, after a student responds to a question, seems to have an even greater impact on the quality of the response because it allows students to organize information, which results in a deeper processing and engagement in formulating their thoughts. More students tend to join the discussion when this kind of wait time occurs. Again, leaders need to practice this strategy so that it becomes natural for them to use it in SI sessions. They will find that the quality of student responses will improve if they use this technique.

Of course, checking for understanding is essential. If the leader simply asks the students if they have any questions or if they had trouble understanding a difficult concept, they may just say no. But the leader should not assume that this response is accurate. Therefore, the leader needs to devise a strategy that engages the students in demonstrating what they know and how they know it. The leader can ask open-ended questions that require students to explain in their own words that they understand a difficult concept before the leader moves on to the next topic. The leader may ask students to summarize the concept that was just covered, write the main points or steps to a problem on the board, give an application of the concept, or write about or demonstrate a similar problem (University of Missouri-Kansas City, 2004).

Problem-Solving SI Strategies. Courses such as math, chemistry, and physics may present significant challenges for students. They may not know where to start in solving a problem, or it may have been many years since they last took this kind of course. Faculty may not have the time or opportunity to address effective problem-solving strategies in class. Therefore, SI can provide an environment in which students can grapple with difficult problems and work together to improve their skills. SI offers the benefit of collective thinking and problem solving. Students can share what they know, ask the leader for input if needed, and collaboratively come up with the sequence of steps and usage of formulas to arrive at the correct answer to a problem.

Boardwork is essential in processing the steps and arriving at a solution. Student pairs can write on small whiteboards to work through a problem and then demonstrate the problem for the whole group. It is essential to include enough time for the student teams to present how they thought about the problem, the steps involved, and how they arrived at the solution. The *Supplemental Instruction Leader Resource Manual* (University of Missouri-Kansas City, 2004) contains a boardwork model that clearly illustrates the techniques described here.

SI strategies for understanding course content in the humanities and social sciences differ from problem-solving techniques (University of Missouri-Kansas City, 2004). An effective strategy to employ here is to analyze the complexity of a concept or the link between various theories or thought processes. While verbalizing or writing may be the common currency in a humanities presentation, organizing vast amounts of material may be more important in a social sciences course. The leader thus needs to structure the SI session plan so that students engage with the material in the way that the professor wants them to. The SI leader has usually taken the professor's course and mastered the strategies that work effectively. It is a good idea for leaders to share how they think about a concept. This modeling can help students apply critical thinking and analysis for themselves.

Organizing information from both the lectures and textbooks is key to mastering content in social science courses such as history. Providing handouts such as matrices or other visual models and having students use them to think about and process information with a partner or in a small group forces them to use their notes, discuss key elements, and demonstrate an organizational pattern that clearly illustrates their understanding of the content.

Conclusion

SI gives students a chance to continue the learning that begins in the classroom and take ample time to struggle with concepts and ideas, work through difficult material, develop effective thinking and processing strategies, and benefit from the synergy of a group working together to solve problems and more effectively engage with difficult material. This model, which has been used for more than thirty years, still yields strong results in student learning, higher final course grades, and lower DFW rates across disciplines, types of colleges, and student ethnicities. In 1981, the U.S. Department of Education designated SI as a model postsecondary retention program and advocated its dissemination throughout the United States (Blanc, DeBuhr, and Martin, 1983). It is a viable retention program that continues to be used as a solid intervention in colleges and universities around the world.

References

Apple, M. *Teachers and Texts*. New York: Routledge, 1988.
Ausubel, D. P. *Learning Theory and Classroom Practice*. Toronto: Ontario Institute for Studies in Education, 1967.
Bakhtin, M. *Toward a Philosophy of the Act*. Austin: University of Texas Press, 1993.
Bandura, A. *Social Learning Theory*. Englewood Cliffs, N.J.: Prentice Hall, 1977.
Blanc, R. A., DeBuhr, L., and Martin, D. C. "Breaking the Attrition Cycle: The Effects of Supplemental Instruction on Undergraduate Performance and Attrition." *Journal of Higher Education*, 1983, *54*(1), 80–89.
Bruner, J. S. *Processes of Cognitive Growth: Infancy*. Worcester, Mass.: Clark University Press, 1968.
Doyle, W. "Academic Work." *Review of Educational Research*, 1983, *53*(2), 159–199.
Epstein, R. (ed.). *Skinner for the Classroom: Selected Papers*. Champaign, Ill.: Research Press, 1982.
Erickson, R. "Taught Cognitive Learning in its Immediate Environment: A Neglected Topic in the Anthropology of Education." *Anthropology and Education Quarterly*, 1982, *13*, 149–180.
Flower, L., and Hayes, J. R. "A Cognitive Process Theory of Writing." *College Composition and Communication*, 1981, *32*, 365–387.
Freire, P. *Pedagogy of the Oppressed*. New York: Continuum, 1988.
Geertz, C. *Local Knowledge: Further Essays in Interpretive Anthropology*. New York: Basic Books, 1983.
Herbart, J. F. *The Science of Education, Its General Principles Deducted from Its Aim, and the Aesthetic Revelation of the World*. (H. Felkin and E. Felkin, trans.) Boston: Heath, 1895.
Hurley, M. "Video-based Supplemental Instruction (VSI): An Interactive Delivery System That Facilitates Student Learning." Unpublished doctoral dissertation, Department of Urban Leadership and Policy Studies in Education, University of Missouri-Kansas City, 2000.
Johnson, D., Maryuyama, G., Johnson, R., Nelson, D., and Skon, L. "The Effects of Cooperative, Competitive and Individualistic Goal Structure on Achievement: A Meta-Analysis." *Psychological Bulletin*, 1981, *89*, 47–62.

Kozol, J. *Amazing Grace: The Lives of Children and the Consciousness of a Nation.* New York: Crown, 1995.

Piaget, J. *The Moral Judgment of the Child.* New York: Free Press, 1973. (Originally published in 1932.)

Riley, J.P. "The Effect of Preservice Teacher's Cognitive Questioning Level and Redirecting on Student Science Achievement." *Journal of Research in Science Teaching,* 1981, *11*(2), 81–94.

Rowe, M. B. "Wait-Time and Rewards as Instructional Variables: Their Influence on Language, Logic, and Fate Control: Part 1—Wait Time." *Journal of Research in Science Teaching,* 1974, *11*(2), 81–94.

University of Missouri-Kansas City. *Supplemental Instruction Leader Resource Manual.* Kansas City: Curators of the University of Missouri, 2004.

University of Missouri-Kansas City. *Supplemental Instruction Supervisor Manual.* Kansas City: Curators of the University of Missouri, 2005.

Vygotsky, L. S. *Thought and Language.* (A. Kozulin, trans.) Cambridge: Massachusetts Institute of Technology Press, 1986. (Originally published in 1934.)

MAUREEN HURLEY *is associate director of and a certified SI trainer for the Center for Academic Development and the International Center for Supplemental Instruction at the University of Missouri-Kansas City.*

GLEN JACOBS *is director of and a certified SI trainer for the Center for Academic Development and the International Center for Supplemental Instruction at the University of Missouri-Kansas City.*

MELINDA GILBERT *is a student in the master's program in counseling and guidance and a graduate intern at the Center for Academic Development and the International Center for Supplemental Instruction at the University of Missouri-Kansas City.*

3

This chapter describes how a well-respected peer-led academic support model, Supplemental Instruction (SI), has been successful in improving grades and reducing failure in high-risk courses at LaGuardia Community College since 1993.

Supplemental Instruction at a Community College: The Four Pillars

Joyce Ship Zaritsky, Andi Toce

Supplemental Instruction (SI) is a recognized and highly respected academic support program available worldwide in institutions of higher learning (Martin and Arendale, 1990; Martin, Arendale, and Associates, 1992; Ogden and others, 2003). Outcomes have demonstrated that SI can contribute to significant change in students' performance by raising grades and reducing failure in high-risk courses.

SI was first piloted at LaGuardia Community College in 1993 with three courses. By 2002–03 the program had expanded to target and support one hundred courses (Zaritsky, 1994, 1998, 2001). There have been 136 participating instructors and 234 SI leaders in LaGuardia's SI program since its inception. This indicates that of the 234 leaders in the program's history, 184 are former leaders, and 50 are current leaders. Data collected during this time show that students who attend SI sessions achieve, on average, one letter grade higher than those who do not attend. (See Table 3.1.)

The data also show that students who participate in SI are less likely to drop the targeted course and therefore more likely to persist. Over the years since program inception, we have also learned that running a successful SI program on our campus depends on the support of four interdependent groups, or pillars: SI supervisors, SI leaders, faculty, and administration.

NEW DIRECTIONS FOR TEACHING AND LEARNING, no. 106, Summer 2006 © Wiley Periodicals, Inc.
Published online in Wiley InterScience (www.interscience.wiley.com) • DOI: 10.1002/tl.230

23

Table 3.1. Classes, Students, SI Participation, and Grade Comparisons at LaGuardia Community College, 1993 to 2005

Semester+	Classes Supported	Total Students	SI Students ****	Participation (%)	Grade Difference**	Rating (%)***
Spring 1993*	3	90	40	44.44	1.30	88.00
Fall 1993*	3	124	55	44.35	1.30	88.00
Spring 1994*	3	113	56	49.56	1.30	88.00
Fall 1994*	6	208	85	40.87	1.30	87.00
Spring 1995*	8	336	143	42.56	1.30	95.00
Fall 1995*	6	343	150	43.73	0.69	88.00
Spring 1996	12	406	172	42.36	1.22	89.00
Fall 1996	13	344	146	42.44	1.19	94.00
Spring 1997	13	342	158	46.20	1.31	85.00
Fall 1 1997	13	392	156	39.80	1.15	89.00
Fall 2 1997*	1	24	20	83.33	1.30	88.00
Spring 1998	12	323	131	40.56	1.34	84.00
Fall 1 1998*	10	313	131	41.85	1.30	88.00
Fall 2 1998*	1	24	20	83.33	1.30	88.00
Spring 1 1999*	12	300	120	40.00	1.30	88.00
Fall 1 1999	8	280	104	37.14	1.40	81.00
Fall 2 1999	7	149	92	61.74	1.10	86.00
Spring 1 2000	15	389	159	40.87	1.25	86.00
Spring 2 2000	6	151	76	50.33	1.30	89.00
Fall 1 2000	10	334	157	47.01	1.40	69.00
Fall 2 2000	6	81	51	62.96	1.50	89.00
Spring 1 2001	15	427	235	55.04	1.60	84.00
Spring 2 2001	5	111	51	45.95	1.40	84.00
Fall 1 2001	9	268	155	57.84	1.20	90.00
Fall 2 2001	6	164	69	42.07	1.30	91.00
Spring 1 2002	22	509	239	46.95	1.50	88.00
Spring 2 2002	6	155	60	38.71	1.30	83.00
Fall 1 2002	27	775	259	33.42	1.00	90.00
Fall 2 2002	22	557	228	40.93	0.90	93.00
Spring 1 2003	45	1324	516	38.97	0.82	90.00
Spring 2 2003	11	293	132	45.05	1.40	95.00
Fall 1 2003	24	647	343	53.01	0.90	84.00
Fall 2 2003	7	237	104	43.88	1.30	92.00
Spring 1 2004	16	478	220	46.03	1.10	98.00
Spring 2 2004	8	189	108	57.14	1.20	96.00
Fall 1 2004	17	461	211	45.77	1.12	91.00
Fall 2 2004	6	104	64	61.54	1.64	91.00
Spring 1 2005	25	706	312	44.19	0.81	91.00
Total	439	12,471	5,528	44.33%	1.24	88%

+ An academic year consists of four terms and begins in July with the Spring 2 semester (6 weeks), followed by Fall 1 (12 weeks), Fall 2 (6 weeks), and Spring 1 (12 weeks).
* Some of the data for this semester are estimates.
** A grade difference of 1 equals an increase of one letter grade.
*** Percentage of students who rated the SI sessions "excellent" or "good."
**** Number of students who attended the SI sessions three or more times.

NEW DIRECTIONS FOR TEACHING AND LEARNING • DOI: 10.1002/tl

The SI Model Explained

SI varies in several ways from traditional academic support models. Instead of targeting struggling students, SI targets difficult or "high-risk" courses—those with a failure rate of 30 percent or higher—providing free assistance to all students enrolled in these classes. In addition, by encouraging all students to attend, the model removes the stigma that students feel when they are assigned to academic support programs; it permits all students, even those already doing well, to improve their grades and performance. Finally, in SI sessions, students work in small groups that are structured to facilitate the review and discussion of important concepts and ideas from the course meetings.

SI leaders are trained extensively in workshops that emphasize active learning. During these workshops, they are taught the principles and methodology of collaborative and cooperative learning (Bruffee, 1994; Goodsell and others, 1992; Johnson, Johnson, and Holubec, 1994; Meyers and Jones, 1993) and are expected to apply them. They are taught to regard themselves as facilitators or coaches, not as instructors.

SI leaders are required to attend the targeted class and take notes as if they were students in the course. This helps them stay current with the material that needs to be addressed during their sessions, it allows them more opportunity to be visible to the students, and it ensures that there is always a "good set of notes" to reference in the sessions. They then organize a minimum of three to five hours a week of group study sessions. In this way, they are intimately aware of what is happening in the class, can form a working relationship with the professor, and can provide help directly relevant to the course material. Attending the class also permits SI leaders to get to know students in the course and to encourage them to attend their sessions.

Attendance at SI study sessions is voluntary, which can be a challenge at a community college such as ours given the demographics of our student body. However, we have found that incentives and support from faculty somewhat alleviates this problem.

About LaGuardia Community College

LaGuardia Community College is an urban public institution located in Queens, New York, a borough that calls itself "the most diverse place in the world" since 46 percent of its two million residents hail from more than one hundred other nations ("About Queens," 2005).

The demographics at our college are similar to those of Queens. Furthermore, the majority of our 13,500 credit students come from low-income households: 63 percent live in households with an annual income of $25,000 or less. Some 61 percent receive some financial aid, which is usually not enough to cover all of their expenses. The high cost of living in the New York metropolitan area requires many students to work part-time or full-time. Fifty-nine percent of our students are foreign-born and some need assistance in learning English. Furthermore, LaGuardia is an open-enrollment institution. As a result, 87 percent of our students come to the college with deficiencies in such basic skills as English, math, and reading and must take remedial or developmental courses before they can enroll in content courses. Even after they complete these courses, many still need additional support. Often they have parental or family responsibilities, which may not allow them sufficient time for study.

These demographics often limit our ability to find and hire SI leaders. Therefore, all of the support groups described in this chapter must work together to ensure the program's success.

The First Pillar: SI Supervisors

As supervisors—the first pillar of the program—our role is to provide the leadership and oversight necessary to support the other three pillars. For example, we must ensure that our SI leaders are carefully chosen, trained, supervised, and supported. In addition, we must work with the faculty and the college administration (their roles are explained in greater detail later in this chapter).

Our program staff is made up of only three part-time individuals. The director is a faculty member who is given two-thirds release time for this position. She oversees and generally supervises the program planning, hires SI leaders, interacts with the administration and faculty, and writes the biannual grant reports and the annual application for funds.

The program assistant is a former student and SI leader who works half-time for the program. His role is to assist the director in her responsibilities. He is in charge of compiling and analyzing the data we produce each semester. In addition, with the oversight of the director, he develops the annual budget for our operation and periodically updates our Web site (http://www.lagcc.cuny.edu/api).

There is also a part-time secretary, who works a total of six hours a week for the program. Her primary responsibility is to make sure that our SI leaders are paid.

Administrative expenses represented only 28 percent of our budget for the 2004–05 academic year. In addition, whenever we have received additional funding, we have put it directly into program expenses, without adding any administrative staff or costs.

The Second Pillar: SI Leaders

Our SI leaders are an essential pillar of our program. At an urban community college such as LaGuardia, choosing and retaining them are continual challenges. It can be difficult for students to take a part-time job as an SI leader, which requires ten to thirteen hours a week and pays between $1,026 and $1,190 for a twelve-week semester. Students may instead need better-paying, off-campus jobs that are readily available in New York. It is also difficult to find students whose communication skills are sufficient for the task.

Selecting SI Leaders. Our recruiting process generally takes a three-pronged approach. First, we recruit on campus with fliers, on our Web site, and through e-mail correspondence to all Honor Society members. Second, we ask all faculty and SI leaders who have worked with us to recommend outstanding students. Third, we highlight our minimum criteria in all of our recruiting information. Candidates must have the following: (1) a 3.0 GPA or higher, (2) a B+ in the course for which they wish to be an SI leader, (3) a minimum of ten to twelve hours a week available for an on-campus position, and (4) a desire to help other students.

Hiring SI Leaders. Our hiring process involves three steps: an interview, a review of each candidate's college transcript, and a check of references.

When applicants appear, they are asked to read a one-page explanation of LaGuardia's SI program and then complete a brief application. If they meet our criteria, we set up an appointment for an interview. The interview is designed to give us information about each student's background and a sense of the student's empathy and friendliness. Because attendance at SI study sessions is voluntary, we have found that outgoing, friendly student leaders are more likely to attract participants. However, we have hired quiet students with good qualifications who have blossomed as a result of their experiences with the program.

During the interview we ask candidates these questions: *Why do you want to become an SI leader? How did you find out about SI? What are your career goals? In what courses are you interested in leading SI? What are your off-campus responsibilities?* This last question is most important; from past experience, we have learned that students with heavy off-campus commitments do not have enough free time to be able to fulfill their responsibilities as SI leaders. We conclude the interview by telling students that we will check their transcripts and references and notify them if they have been selected.

In addition to carefully checking their transcripts, we also look at the candidates' academic patterns, such as a high course withdrawal rate. We do not summarily eliminate these candidates, but we do call them back to inquire about these issues to determine if we feel they can carry out the necessary duties.

We check references from two different sources: faculty and outside employers. Faculty references are vital; they can reveal far more than course grades. It is an extremely positive indication that a student will be an exemplary SI leader if a faculty member reports that the candidate voluntarily assisted other students in the class. Outside references are usually positive; nevertheless, they help us ascertain a candidate's sense of responsibility and reliability in a job setting. If the reference is from a current employer, we find out the time commitment that position entails. As already mentioned, we know that a student who is working many hours for an outside employer (forty to fifty hours, for example) and is also enrolled as a full-time student will not be able to perform well as an SI leader.

Based on the interview, the transcript, and the reference checks we create a pool of prospective candidates. We have learned to compile a ranked list of possible SI leaders that is at least one-third longer than we need. In this way, should one or more candidates drop out at the last minute, we have alternates.

Training SI Leaders. There is sufficient evidence that if SI leaders are to be effective they must be well trained (Cooper and Marie, 2002; Peterman, 2003; Whitman, 1988). For this reason, we provide a good deal of training, starting with a two-day intensive workshop prior to the semester.

The objectives of training are to: (1) introduce students to how SI works; (2) help students understand the nature of SI and how it is different from other academic support programs; (3) introduce students to basic theories of learning; (4) model and have them practice strategies associated with cooperative and collaborative learning; (5) review various study skills; (6) discuss behavioral issues they may encounter and how they may approach them; and (7) view and analyze videotapes of exemplary SI sessions. We use the SI leader training materials that have been developed at the University of Missouri-Kansas City (1997) and a manual that we developed on our own.

The training is continued and reinforced during the semester in weekly ninety-minute meetings. At these meetings, SI leaders also share their successes and concerns—learning experiences in themselves. In addition, each semester the director and the program assistant observe all SI leaders and meet with them to discuss their sessions and provide constructive criticism on session improvement. We also require our SI leaders to observe each other and follow up their observations with similar meetings.

Benefits to SI Leaders. Although academic support programs such as ours often measure the improvement students achieve, they may overlook the important influence SI has on the leaders themselves. To measure the effects of our program in April 2005, we mailed a survey to all of the 184 former SI leaders. We received forty completed surveys (a return of 22 percent, which is considerably high given the great mobility of our student body) and learned the following information:

- Ninety-five percent of respondents reported that SI was very helpful in giving them a better understanding of the course material.
- Seventy-three percent reported that their work as SI leaders helped them choose a career. A large number told us that they had decided on a career in academia—getting a Ph.D. and becoming university faculty—because of their experiences as SI leaders. SI helped them discover the pleasure of helping others and improved their skills as educators.
- Ninety-eight percent reported that being an SI leader helped them gain self-confidence. SI gave them the opportunity to strengthen their leadership and communication skills. Most of them wrote some variation of this

comment: "I was very reluctant to speak in public or express my ideas in front of an audience. Through SI, I was able to break that barrier and open up more."

In their concluding comments, almost all respondents unanimously described SI as "a life-changing experience," "a wonderful program," "the best thing that ever happened to me at LaGuardia." They commented that they considered the program "an extremely valuable teaching tool" that should be implemented in all colleges.

The Third Pillar: The Faculty

The third important pillar of our SI program is our faculty. We have learned that SI works best when faculty understand and support the program. It is therefore essential to choose faculty who view themselves as "gate openers" rather than "gatekeepers," because the former are more likely to support the program by encouraging students in their classes to attend the study sessions.

Before assigning SI leaders to specific courses, we meet with individual faculty, provide them with ample literature on SI, and request their participation. In this way, faculty do not feel they are being required to participate and are more likely to support the program. We also try to match SI leaders to faculty they have studied with and know and respect. This is not always possible at our college, and there are times when we need to assign SI leaders to adjunct professors who are not familiar with the program. In this case, we provide the SI leader with an introductory letter and literature about SI to give to the faculty member on the first day of class. Although this practice is not preferred, in the twelve years we have been running SI at our college we have never had a faculty member turn away an SI leader.

We ask faculty to encourage their students to attend SI sessions. Attendance is a significant issue since it is voluntary. Our students have little free time and may not want to attend SI sessions unless it is clear that doing so will improve their grades. Our strongest faculty encourage their students to attend sessions in several ways: they constantly mention SI in class and include it in their syllabi, they use the SI leader as an assistant whenever there is group work in class, they offer a small amount of extra credit to students who attend more than a minimum number of SI sessions, and they provide materials and support to SI leaders by meeting with them on a weekly basis to review and suggest material and topics they can use in their sessions. We have developed a growing list of "gate-opening faculty" and try as much as possible to assign SI leaders to their classes.

During the semester, we keep in constant communication with faculty through e-mail, invite them to our meetings, and send them agendas as well as copies of some of the training materials. At the end of the semester, we ask participating faculty to complete a survey in which they evaluate both their

SI leader and the program and offer comments and suggestions. Most are extremely enthusiastic in their evaluations. We share our SI data outcomes, which provide them with important feedback and is another incentive to encourage them to participate in the future. We also invite faculty to our annual end-of-year ceremony in which we honor them as well as the students who have worked as SI leaders. We know that many faculty are enthusiastic about the program because of the frequent calls we receive from them requesting that an SI leader be assigned to their classes.

The Fourth Pillar: College Administration

The fourth pillar of our program is the college administration. We rely on their support and are in constant contact by including them in all our e-mails, memos, and invitations. We invite them to all training meetings and events we sponsor. The president and other administrators often come and speak with our SI leaders. In addition, representatives from administration speak each year at our end-of-year ceremony.

By sharing our end-of-semester data, we give administration numerical evidence that the program works and is producing results (see again Table 3.1). We also provide them with data that show that SI need not be considered an additional cost but instead represents an economic savings since the cost of running our program is modest. The college loses approximately $2,000 in state aid for each student who drops out. During the 2004–05 academic year (Spring 2 2004, Fall 1 2004, Fall 2 2004, Spring 1 2005), we targeted fifty-six sections in which 1,460 students were enrolled in courses supported by SI sessions. This worked out to a cost of $72 per attendee.

Funding since the inception of the program has come primarily from our institution's annual state and federally funded Carl D. Perkins Vocational and Technical Act Grant. As an indication of our administration's support, we have received an increase in funding. From time to time, the administration has also provided us with additional funds from its tax levy budget.

The administration's support is vital and should not be overlooked. Student support services are an important part of the budget at a community college, and we know that we must compete for funding with many other support programs.

Conclusion

There are many challenges in running a successful SI program at an urban community college such as LaGuardia. Despite these challenges, we have learned that with continuing refinement our SI program can have a positive impact on both students and SI leaders. As we have shown, our success has been dependent on four pillars of support that are intrinsically related to each other—each one having an effect on the other.

References

"About Queens." *Queens Almanac*, 2005. http://queens.about.com/od/queensalamanc/f/population.htm. Accessed 2004.

Bruffee, K. A. *Collaborative Learning*. Baltimore, Md.: Johns Hopkins Press, 1994.

Cooper, S., and Marie, A. "Classroom Choices for Enabling Peer Learning." *Theory into Practice*, 2002, *41*(1), 53–57.

Goodsell, A., Maher, M., Tinto, V., Smith, B. L., and MacGregor, J. (eds). "Collaborative Learning: A Sourcebook for Higher Education." University Park:, Pennsylvania State University, 1992.

Johnson, W., Johnson, R. T., and Holubec, E. J. *The Nuts and Bolts of Cooperative Learning*. Edina, Minn.: Interaction Books, 1994.

Martin, D. C., and Arendale, D. R. *Supplemental Instruction: Improving Student Performance, Increasing Student Persistence*. Kansas City: University of Missouri, 1990.

Martin, D. C., Arendale, D. R., and Associates. *Supplemental Instruction: Improving Student Performance, Increasing Student Persistence*. Columbia: National Resource Center for the Freshman Year Experience and Students in Transition, University of South Carolina, 1992.

Meyers, C., and Jones, T. B. *Promoting Active Learning: Strategies for the College Classroom*. San Francisco: Jossey-Bass, 1993.

Ogden, P., Thompson, D., Russell, A., and Simons, C. "Supplemental Instruction: Short- and Long-Term Impact." *Journal of Developmental Education*, 2003, *26*(3), 2–8.

Peterman, D. S. "Student Peer Mentoring in Community Colleges." *Community College Journal of Research and Practice*, 2003, *27*(3), 255–58.

University of Missouri-Kansas City. *Supplemental Instruction Supervisor Manual*. Kansas City: Curators of the University of Missouri, 1997.

Whitman, N. A. *Peer Teaching: To Teach Is to Learn Twice*. ASHE-ERIC Higher Education Report No. 4. Washington, D.C.: Association for the Study of Higher Education, 1988.

Zaritsky, J. S. *Supplemental Instruction: A Peer Tutoring Program at LaGuardia Community College, Long Island City, N.Y.* ERIC Clearinghouse for Community Colleges, ERIC Document Reproduction Service, 1994. (ED 373 850).

Zaritsky, J.S. "Supplemental Instruction: What Works, What Doesn't." In D. C. Mollise and C. T. Matthews (eds.), *Selected Conference Papers, National Association for Developmental Education (NADE), 22nd Annual Conference*, Atlanta, 1998, *4*, 54–56.

Zaritsky, J. S. "Supplemental Instruction at an Urban Community College." In J. E. Miller, J. E. Groccia, and M. S. Miller (eds.), *Student Assisted Teaching: A Guide to Faculty-Student Teamwork*. Bolton, Mass.: Anker, 2001.

Joyce Ship Zaritsky *has been the director of the Supplemental Instruction program at LaGuardia Community College since 1993. She is also a professor in the Department of Communication Skills at the college.*

Andi Toce *is assistant to the director of the Supplemental Instruction program at LaGuardia Community College. He is a graduate student in computer science at CUNY's Queens College and also serves as an adjunct in the mathematics department at LaGuardia.*

New Directions for Teaching and Learning • DOI: 10.1002/tl

4

*This chapter describes key components in the design of a
training course for SI leaders. It describes course content
and accompanying theoretical frameworks, and explains
how content is delivered.*

A Credit-Bearing Course for Training SI Leaders

Sally A. Lipsky

Adequate training of peer staff members is a vital component of successful
peer assistance programs (Hock, Schumaker, and Deshler, 1995; Casazza
and Silverman, 1996; Arendale, 2001; Boylan, 2002). Comprehensive training is particularly important for success in Supplemental Instruction (SI)
programs because the student leaders assume greater job responsibilities
than in other peer assistance programs. According to Deanna Martin
(Burmeister, 1996), the single most common reason for the failure of an SI
program is the lack of consistent training and supervision for the leaders.
Implementing a credit-bearing course for training SI leaders bolsters both
the consistency and the efficacy of the training, especially when successful
completion of the course is required *before* the start of their paid positions.
Through a comprehensive training course, SI leaders receive a foundation
in the learning process and communication skills, as well as practice observing and leading peer sessions. As a result, they begin their jobs with greater
preparedness and confidence, which not only strengthens overall efficiency
and quality of programming but also lessens the need for intense supervision at the beginning of the semester.

Components of Course Design

Several elements are recommended in the development of an effective training course for SI leaders (McLaren, 1999).

New Directions for Teaching and Learning, no. 106, Summer 2006   © Wiley Periodicals, Inc.
Published online in Wiley InterScience (www.interscience.wiley.com) • DOI: 10.1002/tl.231

Accreditation. When the training course bears credit it communicates to students—as well as to faculty and administrators—that academic substance is associated with the content, and therefore, that the course is worthy of serious, committed effort. Furthermore, when they receive course credit participating students are rewarded for their efforts.

Clear Course Goals and Objectives. Course goals and objectives should be clearly defined, measurable, and mirror the knowledge and skills needed for the SI leader positions. When course objectives closely relate to course content, outcomes can be assessed. For example, a typical course goal is: "To prepare selected students for the role of a paraprofessional Supplemental Instruction (SI) leader at the college level." Some sample course objectives are as follows:

Students will describe the purposes and impacts of the SI leader role.
Students will demonstrate an understanding and application of active, collaborative learning techniques.
Students will demonstrate an understanding and application of specific strategies for assisting other students in effectively and efficiently learning subject-related content.
Students will demonstrate an understanding and application of methods for incorporating critical thinking and problem solving into SI sessions.
Students will demonstrate effective communication and group leadership skills.
Students will observe, describe, and critique elements of effective SI sessions.
Students will demonstrate knowledge of how to deal with a diverse group of students, including appropriate resources and agencies for referring students.
Students will assess their trial performance as SI leaders.

Concurrent SI Services. Having students observe and critique other sessions is a valuable part of the course. Thus, the course should run concurrently with an active SI program.

Flexibility. A one-credit (fifteen-hour) course has built-in flexibility: it can be scheduled throughout the entire semester (one hour per week) or during any part of it (three hours per week for five weeks or two hours per week for half the term). In addition, prospective SI leaders are more likely to be able to add a one-credit course to their busy schedules.

Content of the Course

The content of the SI leader training course reflects the learning processes on which Supplemental Instruction is based and which have led to its long-standing success as a model of academic support and retention. Topics are presented in the context of related learning theories and models so that prospective SI leaders become acquainted with the theoretical elements of the recommended practices. When course content progresses from theoretical frameworks to practical strategies, students develop a deeper under-standing and appreciation of the very learning processes that they will employ in their SI leader positions.

The Role of the SI Leader. The initial topic covered is the SI leader's role, as viewed using Knowles's (1984) principles of *andragogy*—that is, learning as adults. The primary role of an SI leader is to guide students away from teacher-directed, dependent learning (that is, child-oriented learning) toward self-directed, independent learning (adult-oriented learning). An SI leader is a peer facilitator as opposed to an instructor or expert. Instead of lecturing or readily giving information to students, the function of an SI leader is to provide structure, direction, and reinforcement in how to learn course content.

Knowles (1984) characterizes adult learners as increasingly self-regulating and independent; possessing a wide range of academic and personal experiences; directing learning toward personal and career interests; focusing increasingly on thinking critically and solving problems; and expecting relevant, tangible progress and immediate application of knowledge and skills learned. With these characteristics as a backdrop, the course outlines methods for incorporating adult learning strategies into peer-led sessions. For example, SI leaders explore ways to use their students' experiences as a valued resource for both planning the content of sessions and engaging students during sessions. Furthermore, SI leaders consider ways to include high-interest activities and immediate transfer of knowledge in sessions.

Introduction to these elements of andragogy leads to the overall theme of the course: elements of effective SI sessions. Course activities, which build on this theme, include identifying, categorizing, and prioritizing the characteristics of effective SI sessions through readings, discussion, role playing, and observation and critique of current SI sessions. In addition, prospective SI leaders practice applying the key elements of effective sessions in their own simulated sessions. In the culminating course activity, each person leads a small-group session; this is followed by a debriefing with the instructor. Afterward, each writes a critique of his or her initial performance in the role of SI leader with reference to the elements of effective SI sessions.

Collaborative Learning. Collaborative learning is a fundamental component of Supplemental Instruction. The constructivist model, which emphasizes learning as an interdependent and social process, provides the framework by which to view this course topic (Casazza, 1998). When working in a collaborative setting, students bring experiences and backgrounds that mold and strengthen their learning (Arendale, 1997). Course content includes methods for establishing collaborative and cooperative learning in sessions, ways to manage groups of students, and techniques to maintain the appropriate level, pace, and content quality in sessions.

Active Learning. Intertwined with the topic of collaborative learning is the topic of active learning. Active learning is essential to SI's mission: to assist students with learning difficult subject content. As peer facilitators for learning, future SI leaders should be prepared to demonstrate and recommend appropriate ways to approach complex subject matter. This topic is introduced by using the model of how learners process information (Arendale, 2002; Casazza, 1998; Dembo, 2001):

- *Step One*: Learners receive information via senses.
- *Step Two*: Learners sort out information in working memory.
- *Step Three*: Learners use information immediately, *or* learners store information in long-term memory for later use.

Step Two—learners sort out information in working memory—is key to SI. In the sessions, students review content from course lectures, readings, and assignments, deciding what information is important. Also, Step Three—learners store information in long-term memory for later use—is significant because in the sessions students work on activities that check for and reinforce understanding and remembering of information for upcoming course exams. Thus, included in the training course are the varieties of active learning strategies that help students select, sort, clarify, organize, store, and ultimately retrieve information from long-term memory. For example, prospective SI leaders are introduced to the value of reviewing and summarizing lecture notes as a group, using idea maps, time lines, and charts to organize information, and using a variety of sensory modes to improve retention.

The training course introduces prospective SI leaders to the many multisensory, hands-on activities they can use in sessions, such as demonstrations and role playing to clarify concepts, puzzles and games to review and reinforce content, presentations in which students teach one another, and activity stations for rotating groups of students.

Incorporating Learning Strategies with Subject Matter. Besides the components of active learning and the connection between increased activity and increased understanding and memory, course lessons focus on the importance of integrating learning strategies with subject matter. Combining "how to learn" with "what to learn" is an essential element of effective peer assistance (Arendale, 2004; Simpson, Stahl, and Francis, 2004). Prospective SI leaders should know about a variety of active learning strategies. Furthermore, they should be able to model the process of self-regulation employed by the adult or "expert" learner—that is, how to choose, use, evaluate, and modify strategies leading to academic success (Weinstein and Stone, 1993). Therefore, during the training course, prospective SI leaders follow the same process of self-regulation that they will be advocating in the sessions they lead (Lipsky, 2004). In other words, the prospective SI leaders do the following:

- Assess their own learning and study strategies in the major topic areas: time management and study environment, goal setting, active listening and note taking, textbook reading, and preparing for and taking tests.
- Demonstrate a familiarity with a range of strategies that they can model and introduce in future SI sessions.

- Observe and critique how experienced SI leaders integrate learning strategies in sessions.
- Practice leading minisessions in which they have incorporated learning strategies with mastery of content material.

Critical Thinking and Problem-Solving Skills. In addition to incorporating learning strategies, SI leaders are expected to integrate critical thinking and problem solving in sessions. College students, especially first-year students, often rely on memorization and literal thinking instead of assimilation and application of information. In the training course, students use Bloom's (1956) taxonomy of educational objectives to reinforce the importance of questioning in the development of higher-level, critical thinking. Course content covers methods for integrating advanced and higher-level questioning activities in peer-led sessions, with the goal of developing students' abilities to think through complex, ambiguous content. Future SI leaders practice the art of questioning and redirecting and the use of open-ended, higher-level questions ("What?" "How?" "Why?") to stimulate thinking and discussion.

Students are also introduced to cognitive process instruction (Lochhead and Clement, 1979) as a model for guiding others in *how* to think. As Deanna Martin noted, at some point in the learning process students "actually have to think about the lesson, to struggle with it" by articulating what they understand, or think they understand, to themselves and their peers (Burmeister, 1996, p. 23). Thus, the course explains the importance of talking through challenging subject matter during the group SI sessions. Activities emphasize ways to create dialogue among students, various communication patterns that can develop in a group, as well as recognition of "talk time" and "downtime."

Learning Assessment. Procedures for assessing learning are another important topic covered in the training course. Given the primary mission of SI—to assist students in learning difficult course content—an aspect often overlooked is whether learning has actually occurred in a session. During this course, SI leaders become aware of methods and tools to generate meaningful evidence of learning, such as using classroom assessment instruments (Cross and Angelo, 1988). Originally intended for classroom instructors, these informal assessment techniques can readily be adapted for use in SI. By administering these instruments at the beginning, middle, or end of a session, SI leaders receive immediate information about the quantity and quality of student learning. They also can use students' answers and comments when planning for future sessions. Furthermore, by completing these instruments, students practice recommended learning techniques, such as summarizing, reflecting, questioning, paraphrasing, predicting, identifying key ideas, and recognizing what they do and do not know. The course offers a sampling of these techniques, as well as other methods for deriving meaningful evidence of learning, such as students developing and answering practice test items, expanding on each other's questions and responses, teaching one another, and creating examples or case studies.

Diversity. The topic of diversity is presented in the context of today's college students, who are a large and diverse group of learners with differing styles, goals, skill levels, backgrounds, values, and prior educational, work, and personal experiences (Angus and Greenbaum, 2003). Differences in race, culture, ethnicity, religion, sexual orientation, and values are broached in the training course. Class discussion and role-playing scenarios take into account uncomfortable, hurtful, or even damaging situations that SI leaders might encounter—students making prejudicial remarks, sexist comments, or racial jokes—and how to handle such encounters. Appropriate on-campus and off-campus resources and agencies for referring students with particular problems or concerns are noted.

In addition, the course approaches diversity from the perspective of differences in how students learn—that is, learning styles or preferences. Course content consists of definitions, explanations, and self-awareness of learning styles and the connections between how individuals learn and the choices they make about learning and study behaviors and strategies. As part of the course, SI leaders assess their own learning styles and analyze how their styles affect their choices and approaches toward learning and ways to accommodate differing styles during SI sessions.

Delivery of Course Content

Course content is presented in such a manner as to reflect appropriate instructional and learning strategies for SI sessions. The instructor mimics the same practices and approaches that the SI leaders will be implementing in their positions, including modeling, prompting, and group discovery. Through identifying and analyzing these practices, the students enhance their understanding of how to conduct their upcoming SI sessions.

Presenting Subject Matter in Differing Formats. Like SI sessions, the training course sessions are informative, useful, and yet different from the conventional methods of disseminating information in content-area courses. The instructor employs a range of in-class and out-of-class activities: readings, discussion, role-playing and simulated sessions, grouping students into different formations, students teaching one another, activity stations, collaborative quizzes, and so on.

Breaking Down Complex Subject Matter. To maximize learning of complex topics, information is broken down and presented one chunk at a time with adequate time on task for students to practice, reflect, and receive feedback. Students begin with the activities of reading, observing, and critiquing; this is interspersed with short collaborative exercises. These activities build to a simulation of the SI model—students listen to a taped lecture, taking notes as if they were the SI leader for the course, and planning and practicing leading a session. Students evaluate their own performance, as well as each other's. As already noted, leading a trial session is the culminating course activity. As in SI sessions, class sessions become increasingly less structured as students are expected to assume more responsibility for coursework and learning.

Guiding Students Toward Answers. The instructor employs guided questioning techniques in class, as opposed to just giving answers to students. By asking and eliciting questions, the instructor models the same process of answering questions and solving problems that the SI leaders will employ.

Relating Information to a "Real" Situation. The instructor elicits student examples and applications for course topics. For instance, students identify a personal learning experience that illustrates components of cooperative learning (Arendale, 2004, p. 28). In another activity, students review experienced SI leaders' lesson plans with the purpose of distinguishing elements of adult learning in sessions.

Demonstrating Evidence of Learning. The instructor incorporates a sampling of informal assessments that prospective SI leaders are encouraged to use in their sessions. For example, in the middle of a class session the instructor distributes a variation of the "punctuated lecture" (Cross and Angelo, 1988). Students write their answers to the questions: *How much were you concentrating in the class thus far? Did you get distracted? If so, how did you get your attention back? What are you doing to help you understand and remember the information you are hearing? What do you expect to come next in the second part of the class?* This instrument becomes a means to review content, as well as a method for gauging how effectively students are listening in a class or session. As in an actual SI session, the students share and demonstrate active listening strategies.

Creating a Sense of Community Among Students. Usually, five to eight students are enrolled in sections of the course, which parallels the ideal size of an SI group (University of Missouri-Kansas City, 1996). In class sessions, future SI leaders work in pairs and small groups, with everyone involved in talking and doing. A cohesive, friendly, and trusting group of paraprofessional colleagues is established by the end of the training course.

Encouraging Students to Take Risks. In class, students practice leading collaborative activities and sessions and receive feedback from their peers. Thus, risk taking is an inherent part of the course. As in SI sessions, establishing a comfortable and trusting atmosphere is extremely important. Similar to an SI session, the course instructor sits among the students and conscientiously develops an informal and supportive class atmosphere, an atmosphere that encourages collaboration and risk taking.

Conclusion

A one-credit course is a practical and effective means for delivering comprehensive pretraining for prospective SI leaders. When course content is built on solid theoretical foundations, future SI leaders develop a deeper understanding and appreciation of the practices that they will be employing in their SI leader positions. Furthermore, delivery of course content should model the same approaches toward learning that the leaders will be implementing in their sessions.

References

Angus, K. B., and Greenbaum, J. "Position Statement on Rights of Adult Readers and Learners." *Journal of College Reading and Learning,* 2003, *33,* 122–130.

Arendale, D. R. "Supplemental Instruction (SI): Review of Research Concerning the Effectiveness of SI from the University of Missouri-Kansas City and Other Institutions from Across the United States." In S. Mioduski and G. Enright (eds.), *Proceedings of the 17th and 18th Annual Institutes for Learning Assistance Professionals: 1996 and 1997.* Tucson: University Learning Center, University of Arizona, 1997.

Arendale, D. R. "Effect of Administrative Placement and Fidelity of Implementation of the Model on Effectiveness of Supplemental Instruction Program." Paper presented at the National Association of Developmental Education Conference, Louisville, Ky., Mar. 2001.

Arendale, D. R. "Supplemental Instruction Study Strategies: Using the Information Processing Model." Indiana University of Pennsylvania, 2002. http://www.iup.edu/lec/AcadAssist/SI/IPM-relatedSIstrategies[1].doc.

Arendale, D. R. "Pathways of Persistence: A Review of Postsecondary Peer Cooperative Learning Programs." In I. M. Duranczyk, J. L. Higbee, and D. B. Lundell (eds.), *Best Practices for Access and Retention in Higher Education.* Center for Research on Developmental Education and Urban Literacy, General College, University of Minnesota, Minneapolis, 2004.

Bloom, B. S. (ed.). *Taxonomy of Educational Objectives, Handbook 1: Cognitive Domain.* Reading, Mass.: Addison Wesley, 1956.

Boylan, H. *What Works: Research-Based Best Practices in Developmental Education.* Center for Research in Developmental Education, Appalachian State University, Boone, NC, 2002.

Burmeister, S. "Supplemental Instruction: An Interview with Deanna Martin." *Journal of Developmental Education,* 1996, *20*(1), 22–24, 26.

Casazza, M. E. "Strengthening Practice with Theory." *Journal of Developmental Education,* 1998, *22*(2), 14–20, 43.

Casazza, M.E., and Silverman, S. *Learning Assistance and Developmental Education.* San Francisco: Jossey-Bass, 1996.

Cross, K. P., and Angelo, T. A. *Classroom Assessment Techniques: A Handbook for Faculty.* Ann Arbor, Mich.: National Center for Research on the Improvement of Postsecondary Teaching and Learning, 1988.

Dembo, M. H. "Learning to Teach Is Not Enough—Future Teachers Also Need to Learn How to Learn." *Teacher Education Quarterly,* 2001, *28*(4), 23–35.

Hock, M., Schumaker, J., and Deshler, D. "Training Strategic Tutors to Enhance Learner Independence." *Journal of Developmental Education,* 1995, *19*(1), 18–26.

Knowles, M. S. *The Adult Learner: A Neglected Species.* (3rd ed.) Houston: Gulf Publishing, 1984.

Lipsky, S. *College Study: The Essential Ingredients.* Englewood Cliffs, N.J.: Pearson/Prentice Hall, 2004.

Lochhead, J., and Clement, J. (eds.). *Cognitive Process Instruction: Research on Teaching Thinking Skills.* Philadelphia: Franklin Institute Press, 1979.

McLaren, A. "Designing a Peer Tutor Training Program." In S. Lipsky (ed.), *Selected Proceedings from the 16th and 17th Annual Conferences of the Pennsylvania Association of Developmental Educators.* Hidden Valley and Hershey, Pennsylvania, 1999.

Simpson, M. L., Stahl, N. A., and Francis, M. A. "Reading and Learning Strategies: Recommendations for the 21st Century." *Journal of Developmental Education,* 2004, *28*(2), 2–32.

University of Missouri-Kansas City. *Supplemental Instruction Supervisor Manual.* Kansas City: Curators of the University of Missouri, 1996.

Weinstein, C. L., and Stone, G. "Broadening Our Conception of General Education: The Self-Regulated Learner." In N. Raisman (ed.), *Directing General Education Outcomes.* New Directions for Community Colleges, no. 21. San Francisco: Jossey-Bass, 1993.

SALLY A. LIPSKY is the coordinator of Supplemental Instruction at Indiana University of Pennsylvania.

This chapter discusses Video-based Supplemental Instruction, a variation of the SI model.

Video-Based Supplemental Instruction: Serving Underprepared Students

Maureen Hurley, Kay L. Patterson, F. Kim Wilcox

Video-based Supplemental Instruction (VSI), a learning model developed at the University of Missouri-Kansas City (UMKC) in the early 1990s, assists students in mastering difficult course content while developing and refining their reasoning and critical thinking skills. In looking at researchers' theories and findings on how students learn most effectively in colleges and universities, VSI, based on Supplemental Instruction, stands out as a methodology that provides strategies and tools for academic success. Programs like SI have been shown to positively affect the student academic environment on campus and can also counteract the isolation that may lead to student attrition (Tinto, 1997).

Academic Need

The Boyer Commission in its report on American research universities (Boyer Commission for Educating Undergraduates, 1988) states that the traditional higher education lecture model often fails to meet the needs of students and institutions for success and retention. Students may manage to graduate from college but fail to master the art of effective note taking, textbook comprehension, powerful essay writing, critical thinking, and exam preparation. Attempts have been made at some institutions to address this problem, but often they are temporary, met with resistance, or not given enough planning and time to yield meaningful outcomes.

NEW DIRECTIONS FOR TEACHING AND LEARNING, no. 106, Summer 2006   © Wiley Periodicals, Inc.
Published online in Wiley InterScience (www.interscience.wiley.com) • DOI: 10.1002/tl.232

Supplemental Instruction (SI) is an academic support program that targets traditionally difficult courses. Its goal is to provide peer-led study sessions that help students learn more effectively, raise their grades, and decrease D, F, and withdrawal rates. At UMKC, as well as at other institutions, there are students for whom SI is not sufficient (Martin and Arendale, 1993). These students often fall into the fourth quartile in entry-level scores, high school rank, ACT scores, or college GPA. The VSI delivery system, an inquiry-based learning model, was designed to meet the needs of these students by positioning them squarely in the center of the learning paradigm.

The Relationship Between SI and VSI

Students enrolled in historically difficult courses may be divided into three groups: (1) those who will be successful; (2) those who are on the verge of success or failure; and (3) those who, barring a serious intervention of some kind, will not be successful. SI targets all students, whereas VSI sets its sights on students in the third group.

Dr. Deanna Martin, former director of the Center for Academic Development (CAD) at UMKC, Dr. Gary Widmar, former vice-chancellor for student affairs at UMKC, Dr. Robert Blanc, former director of the Institute for Professional Preparation at UMKC, and Clark Chipman, former regional program officer at the United States Department of Education, had long worked together on methodologies and projects that enhance student learning. They came to understand that SI was not always powerful enough for students in the potentially unsuccessful group. These are students who would likely benefit from SI study sessions but may not consistently participate. Some students simply need the structure of being enrolled in a class that incorporates the SI methodology into the course delivery. Capturing their time means having the opportunity to provide a more intense and immediate review of the course material as well as appropriate modeling of how to study and prepare for historically difficult courses.

SI is academic support *attached* to the targeted course; VSI is academic support *integrated* into the targeted course. SI makes help *available;* VSI makes help *inevitable*. Integrating SI strategies into the course, VSI results in even greater benefits. By not separating the class from the SI sessions, needed structure is added to ensure participation, and at the same time, provides more flexibility in delivering and processing the course content. Because the VSI facilitator is allowed to control the flow of information to the learners, she or he can also pause to check for and sort out the students' understanding of the course material before students are overwhelmed. In traditional lecture courses, many students are lost a few minutes into the lecture and suffer through the classroom experience as an exercise in frustration. Even if SI is attached to the course, it may take days with additional course lectures in between before the student can attend a scheduled SI ses-

NEW DIRECTIONS FOR TEACHING AND LEARNING • DOI: 10.1002/tl

sion. By then, the teachable moment for the student who is struggling may be lost. VSI provides a structure wherein this may be avoided.

The relationship between SI and VSI is not so much in the methods they employ as in the delivery of assistance. VSI is SI in its most intense and deliberate structural form. Some students are unsuccessful not because they lack the ability but because they need more structure than is usually provided in a traditional course.

How the VSI Model Works

In VSI courses, instructors record their lectures on videotape and students enroll in a video section of the class rather than in the traditional lecture section. A trained facilitator guides the students through the processing of the taped lectures and helps regulate the flow of information to the learners. The lectures are stopped and started as needed, allowing the facilitator to determine if students have comprehended one idea before moving on to the next. Students develop essential reading, learning, and study strategies as they master challenging content. Because VSI manages a significant percentage of the students' study time, students develop more proficient skills in writing, note taking, reading, and critical thinking.

Time to think stands out as the element in the contemporary classroom that is most frequently underemployed. In VSI, the deepest learning occurs when the videotape is stopped and students are allowed ample time to think (Martin and Blanc, 1994). They learn to formulate questions like those modeled by their facilitator, make observations, and consider solutions. More importantly, dialogue about key concepts occurs with fellow students and the facilitator. Conflicting ideas are clarified, and differences in opinion are aired and weighed. Students leave the VSI session with the confidence that they understand the main themes and key ideas and can link those to past knowledge.

Kuh (1996) recommends that the following elements be present in order to foster student learning and personal development: a clear and consistently expressed educational purpose, a clear expectation for student performance, use of effective teaching methods, systematic assessment of student performance, and a pervasive learning ethos. These conditions, working in congruence, result in what Kuh refers to as a *seamless learning environment*. According to Kuh, students take much less responsibility for their own learning in lecture-based classes than they do in those with interactive components and study groups. Under the latter conditions, students play a more active role in constructing their own learning. VSI integrates all of these key elements and provides a community in which students meet four to five times a week, usually in two-hour blocks, and work together in small groups.

Learning Strategies Used. Curriculum and classroom design require an understanding of adult learning characteristics and needs. Research shows that adults learn more and feel more comfortable working in small groups and in nontraditional classroom arrangements. Facilitation of student learning is a critical component. To make this happen, Zemke and Zemke (1995) suggest the following elements be present in the classroom: (1) questioning techniques, (2) a comfortable environment, (3) positive reinforcement and feedback, and (4) sensitivity to the needs of the students.

In VSI, these goals are achieved primarily in two ways: by slowing down the pace of the learning and by modeling how to formulate questions that lead to analysis and synthesis. Groups of students are taken off the fifty-minute clock and paired with competent facilitators who "drag their feet." This helps students engage in deeper learning and in processes that can help them become successful in constructing their own knowledge. The facilitator, usually a graduate student or faculty or staff member, is a master student and learner. He or she models successful student behavior such as note taking, reading textbooks, organizing chunks of information into a manageable whole, and preparing for exams. Facilitators are paid a semester based salary comparable to that of an adjunct instructor.

Elements of the Model. The VSI learning model is composed of four elements: preview, process, review, and polish. These components do not necessarily occur in sequence.

In the *preview stage,* the facilitator asks the students what they already know about a topic in order to create a bridge to new content in the lecture or text. Prereading of text material for key concepts and ideas, and writing prenotes may also be part of the preview.

The *process component* is central to VSI and occurs at all stages. Longer class sessions provide more time for students to process the content. The critical time to think is prominent in VSI, but it is frequently absent in college classrooms. VSI students have time to formulate and ask questions, make observations, verbalize areas of confusion, and seek clarification of information from their fellow students. Often they are not skilled in doing this on their own. Therefore, the facilitator is trained to not always answer questions but rather to redirect students to do this for themselves. In this way, students become responsible for their own learning.

For this to work successfully, students need to actually construct a plan of action by which they participate in the process of formulating strategies for success. This occurs regularly in the VSI classroom and in individual meetings with students. According to Brookfield (1990), one of the most critical strategies instructors (or facilitators) can use is to challenge students to reach beyond their comfort level and seek various perspectives.

Review is another ongoing component of the VSI class. An effective facilitator provides opportunities for students to summarize key concepts and discuss how topics are linked. When lectures are stopped, the facilitator is prepared to structure activities that encourage critical thinking and group learning. Students constantly rely on one another to ask questions and formulate answers. They work together on assignments and activities that allow them time to go over difficult material and organize it so they can make sense of their ideas. Formulating exam questions and developing matrices and other visuals can be very helpful to students. It is necessary for them to engage in these practices early and often.

Polish is a VSI element that allows students to refine what they know and finalize their preparation for examinations. By this stage, students should have a thorough grasp of the material and be able to quiz each other and sharpen their test-taking skills. They need to learn to master different types of exam questions. It is important that they understand and have time to practice questions that are formatted like the ones on the exam.

Light (1990) recommends that collaborative learning strategies be used in order for students to achieve higher levels of thinking and greater retention of information. At Harvard, Light (1992) found that group learning worked particularly well in science courses. He discovered that other gains for students came from their engaging in peer review of each other's work. This positively affected their self-confidence and self-esteem.

What student learning comprises, how learning occurs, and how educators can help bring about desired learning in students—all this should be considered in planning for a class (Marchese, 1997). Furthermore, the focus should be on comprehension as well as application and transfer. It is essential that educators look at what methods and strategies help students become better learners and not just if they can apply what they have learned in the short term on an examination.

Program Implementation

Once the course and professor are selected and approved, the planning begins. Some professors deliver their taped lectures just as they would in the classroom; others are willing to build in stops that allow a natural flow for the students to process the material, ask questions, and engage in discussion. The materials that are developed to accompany the course include specific examples of strategies to master specialized content.

VSI students enroll in core curriculum courses for which the professor has recorded his or her lectures on videotape. Students only attend the video section of the course, yet the same rigorous performance standards are maintained for both the regular and the VSI sections. Facilitator and student manuals accompany the video course in order to ensure that these standards are maintained.

Support materials include small group assignments to make certain that learning is achieved before the class moves on to subsequent topics. Students work on these activities and assignments with the guidance of the facilitator.

Study strategies are closely tied to the content, and often students are not even aware that they are developing effective learning tools (Martin and Blanc, 1994; Burmeister, 1996). Students are also encouraged over the course of the semester to think metacognitively—that is, to think about which techniques are most helpful to them in mastering the content.

One of the most important elements of a successful VSI course is the facilitator. Facilitators must be competent in the course content and experienced in leading groups. Before the semester begins, they participate in an intensive two-day workshop. The training models effective learning strategies for them. They then demonstrate activities, employing the techniques they have learned that apply to their disciplines. After the term begins, a vital part of the support continues: ongoing coaching. During the first week, daily activity plans are discussed with the VSI program coordinator, who visits each classroom several times. The facilitator and coordinator discuss how student learning is progressing and plan additional strategies for subsequent sessions. Beginning in the second week of classes, facilitators observe each other's sessions and complete the same observation form.

Biweekly meetings are held with the entire group of facilitators working on various issues related to problem solving and use of appropriate learning strategies. There is much sharing of ideas and approaches to working with students. The coordinator should foster the spirit that all VSI students may need to be helped in some way by the VSI staff.

Teaching sound learning strategies and helping students do well academically are among the goals of VSI. All students who enroll in a VSI class need to understand the time and energy commitment they will be making. Those who have the dedication and time to put into their work will be the most successful. They must be willing to participate in class, work in groups, and complete assignments. It is important for the VSI staff and facilitators to clearly articulate this to the students from the beginning. Course completion, reenrollment, and retention can then follow. Tinto (1997) advocates that retention is a result, not a goal, of a sound approach to academics.

Among the elements of supervision of the VSI program are maintaining ongoing relationships with administrators, advisers, and facilitators. As new VSI courses are developed, communication among department chairs, faculty, and the VSI coordinator is critical and ongoing.

Some students on academic probation are required to enroll in a VSI class in order to be readmitted to the university. As courses such as chemistry, intermediate algebra, and college algebra were added to the mix of VSI courses, student affairs personnel saw the model as a vehicle to support freshmen who needed academic support.

Institutional Support

To develop an effective approach to delivering instruction and promoting student learning, it was important for the UMKC Center for Academic Development (CAD) to obtain administrative support for VSI. Dr. Deanna Martin, with the assistance of a student affairs administrator, approached the Department of History, and asked permission to meet with an assistant professor who had obtained numerous teaching awards and was well respected by faculty and students. He believed that those students who struggled with the course content could become more successful if they learned how to structure their time effectively and incorporate meaningful learning strategies into their studying. He agreed to record one of his courses. The lesson learned from this first pilot was the importance of working through departments and central administration in securing approval and support for the program.

In its pilot stage, VSI began with just one course: Western Civilization. Students who wanted to invest the extra time were eligible to enroll. Funding for the development of the course came from a variety of sources, including the academic and student affairs divisions, private local foundations, and the chancellor's fund for innovation. The main budget costs involved in producing a VSI course are for studio production, duplication of tapes, stipends for professors, student materials, and facilitator and staff salaries.

Since the early 1990s, the following VSI courses have been produced at UMKC: General Chemistry I, Intermediate Algebra, College Algebra, Physics of Everyday Life, and Calculus I. Dr. Kay Patterson, VSI coordinator, has been involved in all phases of course development.

Program Evaluation

At UMKC, the VSI coordinator uses both formative and summative evaluation for program improvement and assessment. The VSI program results include a comparison of the academic progress of VSI students with non-VSI students in the same lecture-based course.

UMKC cumulative data from 1997 through 2005 follow. Two figures are presented for each content area: chemistry, history, and intermediate algebra. The first figure in each set of two (Figures 5.1, 5.3, and 5.5) shows the ACT scores of the VSI group compared to the non-VSI group. In each example, the average of the ACT scores of the VSI group is lower than the average of the non-VSI group.

The second figure in each set (Figures 5.2, 5.4, and 5.6) shows a comparison of the GPA of VSI students and the non-VSI students. The data show that the percentage of VSI students receiving a D or F or withdrawing is lower than that of the non-VSI students. In most cases, even though they had lower ACT scores, the VSI group surpassed the non-VSI group in this latter measure.

Summary

VSI provides an opportunity for students to become both interdependent and independent learners. They exert control over their learning experience by using classroom time on task in a more productive manner. Combining *how to learn* with *what to learn,* structuring the classroom experience in a dynamic, comfortable, experiential environment, and practicing effective course strategies allow deeper learning and an easier transition into the rigors of academic life.

NEW DIRECTIONS FOR TEACHING AND LEARNING • DOI: 10.1002/tl

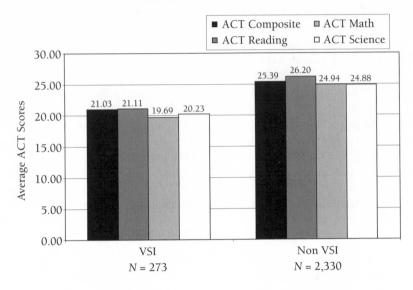

Figure 5.1. Comparison of ACT Scores, Chemistry 211,
Fall 1997 to Fall 2004

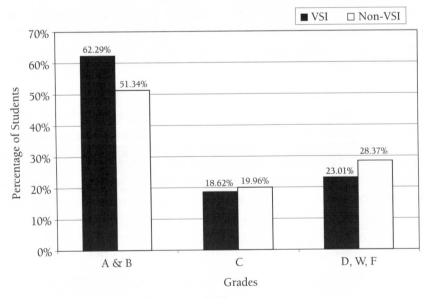

Figure 5.2. Comparison of Grades, Chemistry 211,
Fall 1997 to Fall 2004

Note: VSI students = 278; non-VSI students = 2,572.

Figure 5.3. Comparison of ACT Scores, History 102, Fall 1997 to Fall 2004

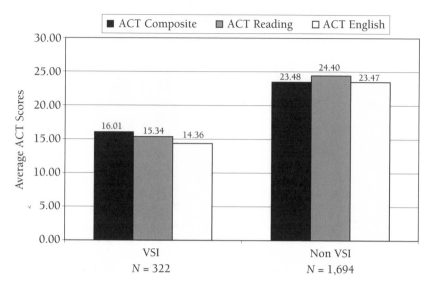

Figure 5.4. Comparison of Grades, History 102, Fall 1997 to Fall 2004

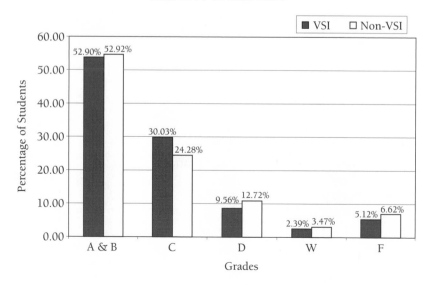

Figure 5.5. Comparison of ACT Scores, Math 110, 1999 to 2004

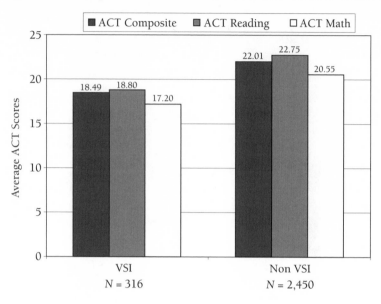

Figure 5.6. Comparison of Grades, Math 110, 1999 to 2004

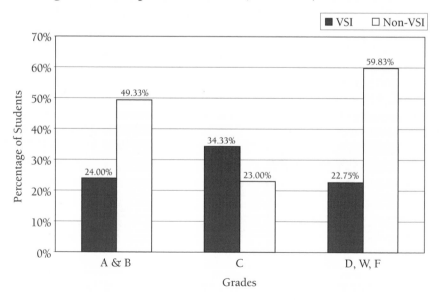

References

Boyer Commission for Educating Undergraduates. *Reinventing Undergraduate Education: Blueprint for American Research Universities.* Washington, D.C.: Heldref Publications, 1988.

Brookfield, S. D. *The Skillful Teacher.* San Francisco: Jossey-Bass, 1990.

Burmeister, S. "Supplemental Instruction: An Interview with Deanna Martin." *Journal of Developmental Education,* 1996, 20(1), 22–24, 26.

Kuh, G. D. "Guiding Principles for Creating Seamless Learning Environments for Undergraduates." *Journal of College Student Development,* 1996, 37(2), 135–148.

Light, R. *Harvard Assessment Seminars: Explorations with Students and Faculty About Teaching, Learning and Student Life.* Vol. 1. Cambridge, Mass.: Harvard Library, 1990.

Light, R. *Harvard Assessment Seminars: Explorations with Students and Faculty About Teaching, Learning and Student Life.* Vol. 2. Cambridge, Mass.: Harvard Library, 1992.

Marchese, T. "A Shift to Learning." *Change,* 1997, p. 4.

Martin, D. C., and Arendale, D. *Supplemental Instruction: Improving First-Year Student Success in High-Risk Courses.* (2nd ed.) Columbia: University of South Carolina and National Center for the First Year Experience and Students in Transition, 1993.

Martin, D. C., and Blanc, R. "Video-Based Supplemental Instruction: A Pathway to Mastery and Persistence." In D. C. Martin and D. Arendale (eds.), *Supplemental Instruction: Increasing Achievement and Retention.* New Directions for Teaching and Learning, no. 60. San Francisco: Jossey-Bass, 1994.

Tinto, V. "Classrooms as Communities: Exploring the Educational Character of Student Persistence." *Journal of Higher Education,* 1997, 68, 599–621.

Zemke, R., and Zemke, S. "Adult Learning: What Do We Know for Sure?" *Training,* June 1995, 31–40.

MAUREEN HURLEY is associate director of and a certified SI trainer for the Center for Academic Development and the International Center for Supplemental Instruction at the University of Missouri-Kansas City.

KAY L. PATTERSON is the VSI coordinator and a certified SI trainer for the Center for Academic Development at the University of Missouri-Kansas City. She has worked with SI and VSI for fifteen years.

F. KIM WILCOX, a certified SI trainer, has been the national coordinator of training for Supplemental Instruction at the University of Missouri-Kansas City for the last fifteen years.

6

This chapter provides a broad overview of the benefits attained by SI leaders as a result of their participation in SI leadership activities.

Benefits to Supplemental Instruction Leaders

M. Lisa Stout, Amelia J. McDaniel

For many years, authors have discussed the benefits of Supplemental Instruction (SI) as they relate to students who attend the sessions. Recently, more practitioners have begun to examine the benefits to those who serve as SI leaders. This chapter reports on how leaders benefit from their experience at the University of Missouri-Kansas City, as well as at other participating institutions. Leaders report academic improvement, increased communication and relationship-building skills, and personal and professional development. These benefits suggest that SI positively affects its leaders as much, if not more than, the students participating in the program.

The *Supplemental Instruction Supervisor Manual* (University of Missouri-Kansas City, 2005) lists the following qualifications for an SI leader: sophomore or higher class standing, cumulative GPA of 3.0 or above, content competency as determined by the course instructor, and sufficient interpersonal skills as determined by the SI supervisor. These are the minimum qualifications; SI supervisors may also give preference to applicants who have attended SI sessions (Wallace, 1992), those who are recommended by experienced SI leaders, those who have themselves struggled with the course material at times, and those who demonstrate flexibility and openness to the learning theory on which SI is based (Martin and Arendale, 1993a). Many students lead SI sessions in their major area of study, but it is not a requirement for becoming an SI leader.

In general, students who appear in their interview to be eager to demonstrate their knowledge of the content material, express interest in

DISCOVER SOMETHING GREAT

NEW DIRECTIONS FOR TEACHING AND LEARNING, no. 106, Summer 2006 © Wiley Periodicals, Inc.
Published online in Wiley InterScience (www.interscience.wiley.com) • DOI: 10.1002/tl.233

being a leader for the sole purpose of reviewing course content, or seem dismissive of students who struggle with issues like time management and note taking should cause concern for the SI supervisor. These attitudes can be addressed in training, but with the average leader training lasting only eight hours it is expedient to select individuals who already believe in supporting educational access for all students, a philosophy on which collaborative learning and the SI model are based. This will allow supervisors to focus on modeling proven SI session strategies and simulating sessions during the training workshop.

Emphasizing particular approaches that are based on sound learning theory during training allows the prospective leaders to practice facilitating student-to-student interaction. Professionals in the field of education understand what a sophisticated task that is, but undergraduate students sometimes underestimate the planning it requires. To assist students in preparing for their leadership role, topics such as group facilitation, study skills, and problem solving are key components of SI leader training (Martin and Wilcox, 1996).

When SI leaders are carefully selected and trained, they experience many unforeseen benefits. Such benefits include increased understanding of the course material, improved communication skills, and enhanced interactions with faculty, students, other SI leaders, and SI staff. In addition, SI leaders experience professional development as a result of formal and informal mentoring by involved faculty and SI staff (Donelan and Kay, 1998; Ashwin, 1994; Donelan, 1999; Wallace, 1992).

Academic Benefits

Although academic improvement should not be a primary motive for students to become SI leaders, it is a positive secondary benefit that students can anticipate (Wallace, 1992). SI leaders often come to the program as strong students, yet they can expect to improve their academic performance after learning and facilitating the student-centered pedagogical practices around which SI is formed (Blanc and Martin, 1994). By continually familiarizing themselves with course material and increasing their understanding of course concepts, a leader's own comprehension of core subject elements and study techniques is improved (Stone, Jacobs, and Hayes, in press). As leaders expand their personal knowledge of academic topics, they are able to bring increased self-confidence and course knowledge to their SI leadership position, thus increasing their image as "experienced learner" (Martin and Wilcox, 1996), a role to which other students can aspire.

In addition to becoming knowledgeable about course content, SI leaders complete many tasks that require data organization and planning. Included in the SI leaders' job description is a substantial amount of time to plan content and processes for each session that they will facilitate. The "Planning an SI Session" sheet prompts leaders to provide a summary of their plan for administrative purposes, but leaders generally prepare a more detailed plan including sample problems. For example, informal quiz questions, one-minute writing questions, and completed matrices are all strategies used by leaders during sessions (University of Missouri-Kansas City, 2004). Because they must complete each activity and solve each problem they plan for their sessions in order to be completely prepared, they learn the material thoroughly.

Furthermore, students from all levels of prior achievement attend SI and contribute to the discussion (Martin and others, 1983), and they often add more details or fresh perspectives to the material that the leader has planned to cover. By spending several hours each week in lecture and planning appropriate cognitive activities for their session, leaders improve their own note-taking skills and study strategies (Ogden, Thompson, Russell, and Simons, 2003; Donelan, 1999).

Session plans, although required, must be flexible enough to accommodate the needs of the students who choose to attend that particular session. Therefore, leaders must be prepared but also be willing to adjust the time spent on each activity based on the progress their students make. Time management is a sophisticated skill that is difficult to teach in one training session. Rather, during session facilitation and throughout the semester, as a student meets his or her own academic obligations and those of being a model student and SI leader, the ability to achieve a productive balance improves with practical experience. Mentors (veteran SI leaders who have been trained in the skills necessary to supervise and coach other leaders), experienced leaders, and SI supervisors guide new leaders in the formation of these skills by observing them regularly and offering structured, specific feedback.

Improved Communication and Relationship-Building Skills

In addition to becoming more sophisticated learners, SI leaders can expect to improve their communication skills and build mature professional and personal relationships. This process is enhanced if leaders are confident in the value of the SI model, have consistent support from their SI supervisor, and have positive peer interaction. This is an excellent reason to select applicants who have actively participated in SI sessions as students. Leaders who have already experienced the benefit of SI for themselves have confidence in the effectiveness of the model, and this encourages them to communicate that feeling to students.

Communication skills learned by SI leaders include setting appropriate boundaries with students, employing the "language of students," and learning to evaluate their students' understanding of material by assessing their body language (Ashwin, 1994). SI supervisors can help leaders refine these skills by observing their sessions regularly and debriefing them promptly. When they observe leaders on a consistent basis, supervisors are better able to hold leaders accountable for fulfilling their responsibilities,

NEW DIRECTIONS FOR TEACHING AND LEARNING • DOI: 10.1002/tl

thus encouraging them to communicate any difficulties they may be having. Just like students who are trying to master difficult content, leaders who are learning how to communicate professionally with peers and faculty need the opportunity to verbalize their struggles and successes.

Most SI leaders come to the program as sophomores or juniors. Although they have had opportunities to interact with faculty and students on a personal level, they may not yet feel comfortable with the communication patterns that successfully build professional relationships. When they participate in the SI program, they must engage in structured activities in order to fulfill their duties as leaders. They have formal and informal interactions with academic experts or faculty who may otherwise intimidate them (Martin and others, 1983; Arendale, 1994). For example, leaders offer to meet with their faculty member at least once each week. These meetings may be formally scheduled or simply occur while walking to or from the lecture. Leaders learn during training that they must solicit feedback from the faculty member about their SI sessions, usually by showing the instructor an activity they have prepared for an upcoming session and asking for their input. This gives them the opportunity to learn to set an informal agenda for meeting with faculty while also providing a structured interaction pattern that can help them gain confidence in their own ideas and ability to make valid contributions to a discussion of content with an expert in the field. Through interaction with faculty, the traditional roles of student and professor are tempered, and students gain the opportunity to participate in meaningful academic relationships with potential mentors (Martin and Wilcox, 1996).

Enhanced Personal Development

The personal benefits of being an SI leader have been noted by several authors. Student recognition of their growing leadership role promotes positive personal development, increased self-confidence, and enhanced self-esteem (for example, Donelan, 1999; Wallace, 1992; Ashwin, 1994; Stone, Jacobs, and Hayes, in press).

Knowing that successful SI sessions depend on a leader who holds each student responsible for the learning of the group, good leaders know they must be assertive in moderating the participation of dominant students and eliciting responses from quieter students. They must be able to set boundaries in the group, not always relying on the supervisor to do so. For example, good leaders feel confident asking for volunteers to go to the board and calling on a student by name if no one volunteers to answer a question. They know that students who are having conversations that are off-task can be disruptive, and they learn that they must approach them and ask them to join the group or risk leading an unproductive session. Accomplishing this difficult task assists in the personal and professional development of the SI leader. As Donelan (1999) noted, "By allowing mistakes and learning from their own and others' misunderstanding and by helping others to make meaningful choices, the leaders facilitate steps towards their own affective and cognitive development towards autonomy" (p. 17).

An SI leader who has mastered the delicate balance of remaining a peer while setting boundaries will likely have well-attended sessions. Soon, that leader will find that he or she has become a minicelebrity on campus. No matter where that individual goes, there are students from SI sessions who wave and say hello. The incidences of "SI leader sightings" increase when leaders stay with the program for more than one semester. Soon, they have a network of friends from all parts of campus.

Furthermore, because SI participants are students of wide-ranging backgrounds (Martin and Arendale, 1993b; Arendale, 1994; Ramirez, 1997; Bidgood, 1994), SI leaders gain the valuable opportunity to interact with diverse student populations. This opportunity promotes increased cultural competency among them, a skill that they can integrate into their SI activities, and ultimately, their broader interpersonal relationships. In addition, their proficiency in issues of diversity will further expand their worldview and help them navigate the continually changing workplace, whether in the campus environment or a corporate setting. Becoming engaged with the campus in this way makes the experience of attending college more positive for leaders, and this in turn increases their sense of self, enabling them to strive to meet their personal, professional, and academic goals.

Enhanced Professional Development

Beyond the academic, facilitation, and personal skills leaders gain from involvement in the SI program, they also enhance their professional development. They gain multiple abilities, including leadership skills (Stone, Jacobs, and Hayes, in press), teamwork strategies (Donelan, 1999), verbal and written expression, and self-assurance (Wallace, 1992). SI leaders thus are able to transfer their abilities from SI sessions to the professional world.

In addition, required paperwork, like participation logs and planning sheets, prompt leaders to keep careful records of their session preparation, attendance, and after-session thoughts. At some institutions, leaders are also responsible for entering their session attendance into a database. Asking leaders to fulfill these administrative duties encourages them to develop skills that are not normally required of students.

The planning rubric, found in the *Supplemental Instruction Leader Resource Manual* (University of Missouri-Kansas City, 2004), asks leaders to estimate the time that each activity will take during the session. Inexperienced leaders often underestimate the time their students will need to master new concepts. As the semester progresses and they get to know their students better, their timing improves. The rubric also asks leaders to consider "worst-case" scenarios and prepare a "Plan B" for those situations: What if only one or two students attend? What if no one brings the text or notes? What if no one has done the assigned reading or homework? By requiring leaders to consider and create contingency plans that focus on productive student-to-student interaction despite a less than ideal learning environment, the SI program nurtures leaders who consider all possibilities, not just the likely, best-case scenario. These skills carry over into preparation for other activities as leaders become SI mentors, officers in SI student organizations, and members of the educated workforce.

As supervisors and mentors observe leaders and debrief their observations, leaders gain experience with performance evaluations and responding to feedback, both positive and negative. The debriefing process always begins with the supervisor asking the leaders how they thought the session went, forcing them to express their view of the session before the supervisor gives his or her impression. Supervisors predominantly practice positive reinforcement and limit their constructive suggestions, targeting only one or two areas for improvement at a time. The leader and supervisor then work together to arrive at specific tactics that will improve the sessions.

Because supervisors do not leave leaders strictly to their own devices or force improvement strategies on them, leaders learn how professionals work together to solve problems. This will serve them as they continue their academic careers or enter team-based corporate environments, or if they advance in the SI program to SI mentor positions. Repeated interactions with faculty expose SI leaders to professional practices in that academic discipline. Thus, the supervisors, faculty members, and mentors who work together with SI leaders to help them develop their professional skills act as role models for the SI leaders. The amount of time leaders spend with SI faculty and staff provide them with the opportunity to build professional relationships founded in specific, shared experiences, ultimately lending an authenticity to leader interactions with faculty and staff.

Although personal gain is not the primary goal of SI leaders, there are definite incentives to SI leadership, such as acquiring faculty letters of reference that are genuine and uniquely personalized. In addition, leaders gain a multitude of opportunities to document in their curriculum vitae (CV), including numerous training sessions and leadership accomplishments (Wallace, 1992; Donelan, 1999). Inclusion of SI leadership on a student's CV indicates to future employers that the student has participated in a program that requires commitment, communication skills, and the ability to establish positive relationships with both peers and those in leadership positions.

SI leaders often also feel increased confidence in their overall ability to help students in the supported course. This positive experience in the field of education may prompt some to consider careers in higher education. Others may be more likely to pursue graduate studies in their chosen field. Ultimately, SI leadership will almost certainly contribute to the leaders' greater success in their professional and personal ambitions.

Conclusion

In conclusion, we have observed that the SI program provides an impressive list of benefits to SI leaders: mastery of course content, improved communication and professional and personal relationship-building skills, mentoring interactions with faculty, students, other SI leaders, and SI staff, and professional development that results from the administrative requirements, performance evaluations, and interaction with role models. There are attractive opportunities for research in this area. We know that leaders go on to enter a variety of careers, but it would be interesting to gather specific data on the ultimate career and academic avenues pursued by leaders and how SI leadership affected these professional aspirations. There is also a dearth of research on the skills leaders feel they gain from faculty, SI staff, and SI peer mentors specifically. Such exploration would allow us to focus on and increase the benefits derived from particular interactions or certain environments.

As we continue to provide quality SI programs for the benefit of our students and institutions, we must remain cognizant of the value of providing and promoting the academic and professional development benefits we offer to our SI leaders. It is a difficult task to develop a program that simultaneously supports both educators and students, but it is one that reaps a multitude of benefits. SI has successfully established itself as such a program. It provides many benefits to institutions of higher education, including to faculty, staff, and the students receiving SI services. However, as recognized by one SI colleague, SI leaders have established themselves as the "real winners" of the SI program (Donelan, 1999, p. 2).

References

Arendale, D. "Understanding the Supplemental Instruction Model." In D. C. Martin and D. Arendale (eds.), *Supplemental Instruction: Increasing Achievement and Retention* (pp. 11–22). San Francisco: Jossey-Bass, 1994.

Ashwin, P. "The Supplemental Instruction Leader Experience: Why Supplemental Is Not Teaching: A Student's Perspective." In C. R. Rust and J. Wallace (eds.), *Helping Students to Learn from Each Other: Supplemental Instruction* (pp. 87–90). Birmingham, England: Staff and Educational Development Association, 1994.

Bidgood, P. "The Success of Supplemental Instruction: Statistical Evidence." In C. Rust and J. Wallace (eds.), *Helping Students to Learn from Each Other: Supplemental Instruction* (pp. 71–79). Birmingham, England: Staff and Educational Development Association, 1994.

Blanc, R. A., and Martin, D. C. "Supplemental Instruction: Increasing Student Performance and Persistence in Difficult Academic Courses." *Academic Medicine,* 1994, 69(9), 452–454.

Donelan, M. "SI Leaders: The Real Winners." Paper presented at the National Conference on Supplemental Instruction, Kansas City, Mo., May 20–22, 1999.

Donelan, M., and Kay, P. "Supplemental Instruction: Students Helping Students' Learning." *Law Teacher,* 1998, 32(3), 287–299.

Martin, D. C., and Arendale, D. "Foundation and Theoretical Framework for Supplemental Instruction." In D. C. Martin and D. Arendale (eds.), *Supplemental Instruction:*

Improving First-Year Success in High-Risk Courses (2nd ed., pp. 41–50). Columbia, S.C.: National Resource Center for the Freshman Year Experience and Students in Transition, 1993a.

Martin, D. C., and Arendale, D. "Supplemental Instruction in the First College Year." In D. C. Martin and D. Arendale (eds.), *Supplemental Instruction: Improving First-Year Success in High-Risk Courses* (2nd ed., pp. 11–18). Columbia: National Resource Center for the Freshman Year Experience and Students in Transition, University of South Carolina, 1993b.

Martin, D. C., Blanc, R. A., DeBuhr, L., Alderman, H., Garland, M., and Lewis, C. "Supplemental Instruction: A Model for Student Academic Support." University of Missouri and ACT National Center for the Advancement of Educational Practices, University of Missouri-Kansas City, 1983.

Martin, D. C., and Wilcox, F. K. "Supplemental Instruction: Helping Students to Help Each Other." In S. Brown (series ed.) and G. Wisker (vol. ed.), *Enabling Student Learning: Systems and Strategies* (pp. 97–101). London: Kogan Page and Staff and Educational Development Association, 1996.

Ogden, P., Thompson, D., Russell, A., and Simons, C. "Supplemental Instruction: Short- and Long-Term Impacts." *Journal of Developmental Education*, 2003, 26(3), 2–8.

Ramirez, G. "Supplemental Instruction: The Long-Term Impact." *Journal of Developmental Education*, 1997, 21(1), 2–9.

Stone, M. E., Jacobs, G., and Hayes, H. "Supplemental Instruction (SI): Student Perspectives in the 21st Century." *Center for Research in Developmental Education and Urban Literacy*, in press.

University of Missouri-Kansas City. *Supplemental Instruction Leader Resource Manual.* Kansas City: Curators of the University of Missouri, 2004.

University of Missouri-Kansas City. *Supplemental Instruction Supervisor Manual.* Kansas City: Curators of the University of Missouri, 2005.

Wallace, J. "Students Helping Students to Learn." *New Academic*, 1992, 1(2), 8–9.

M. LISA STOUT *is assistant to the director of the Center for Academic Development and the International Center for Supplemental Instruction at the University of Missouri-Kansas City.*

AMELIA J. MCDANIEL *is assistant campus SI coordinator and a certified SI trainer for the Center for Academic Development and the International Center for Supplemental Instruction at the University of Missouri-Kansas City.*

7

This chapter offers a case study of the Nelson Mandela Metropolitan University, South Africa, where SI has acted as more than a student academic development program by also addressing faculty and curriculum development.

How Supplemental Instruction Benefits Faculty, Administration, and Institutions

Sandra Zerger, Cathy Clark-Unite, Liesl Smith

Supplemental Instruction (SI) was born in an era when new students—different from traditional students—were being admitted into the academy. Many of these students were not suited to the prevailing educational delivery—two lectures and a lab—according to Postlethwait (2005). Furthermore, the world has changed in the last thirty-five years. Camblin and Steger (2000) state that accelerated technological advances and globalization, along with fewer financial resources, have created an environment of discord in higher education. In addition, students and parents increasingly demand accountability and high quality in higher education. Colleges and universities must address the learning needs of students in the information age or face obsolescence. Faculty development programs are crucial for keeping education relevant. This chapter explains how a successful SI program can support not only students but also the faculty and the institution itself.

Benefits to Faculty

Faculty development must move beyond providing funds for sabbaticals and academic discipline conferences to focus on teaching effectiveness and methodology (Lawler and King, 2000). According to Camblin and Steger (2000), the assumption has been that scholars (faculty members) can easily

NEW DIRECTIONS FOR TEACHING AND LEARNING, no. 106, Summer 2006   © Wiley Periodicals, Inc.
Published online in Wiley InterScience (www.interscience.wiley.com) • DOI: 10.1002/tl.234

self-educate to stay up-to-date on their own and maintain high teaching skills. But this assumption no longer holds in the information age. Today's workers must acquire and use theoretical and analytical knowledge in increasingly sophisticated ways. Knowledge has become so complex that no single individual can be effective alone; employees can be successful only if they collaborate in teams. According to Weaver and Sorrells-Jones (1999), organizations need "to become increasingly flexible and resilient to support innovation and to change quickly in response to market demands. The preferred model is an organization made up of teams" (p. 19). Team members can challenge and correct each other (Sorrells-Jones and Weaver, 1999). Faculty members who were educated based on the individualistic industrial age model benefit from SI training in collaborative techniques.

Many faculty equate good teaching with knowing the content and delivering it well, based on good lecture notes (Brent and Felder, 2000; Camblin and Steger, 2000; Caffarella and Zinn, 1999). For them, improving teaching is equated with revising their lecture notes (Brent and Felder, 2000). Scholarship, or research, is viewed as a means to obtain tenure and promotion. Boyer (1990) argues for a broader definition of faculty scholarship, moving beyond research and publication as the yardstick. He quotes Clark Kerr: "The university is being called upon to educate previously unimagined numbers of students . . . to adapt to and rechannel new intellectual currents" (cited in Boyer, 1990, p. 53). He broadens the definition of scholarship to include the scholarship of discovery (creating new knowledge—the traditional view of scholarship), the scholarship of integration (making connections across disciplines), the scholarship of application (applying knowledge to consequential problems), and the scholarship of teaching (transforming and extending knowledge to students).

Boyer asserts that the scholarship of application and teaching benefit the academic institution by helping it meet its service obligations. In order for there to be scholarship of integration, departments must overcome the disciplinary isolation characteristic of many institutions. Because SI personnel are trained in collaboration and their educational backgrounds span many disciplines, they can provide leadership for collaborative scholarship. SI has always excelled in the application of theory to practice. Leaders and supervisors are trained to make the abstract concrete, to provide application problems and situations for theory presented in lectures. SI constantly works on improving learning and teaching and is obliged to further the scholarship of teaching. SI, consequently, is well suited to meet the needs of the broader definition of scholarship.

Informal Faculty Development. Faculty may view faculty development as remedial—strictly for those who do not know how to teach or research (Boyle and Boice, 1998). They may not perceive a need to improve, not be aware of their teaching problems, overestimate their teaching strengths, or underestimate the usefulness of the teaching methods they use, especially before they participate in faculty development programs

(Skeff and others, 1997). Faculty may have a narrow view of faculty development and define it only as monies for conferences and publications (Eleser and Chauvin, 1998). For such faculty, development may need to be informal. One should never underestimate the value of talk over a cup of coffee. When a coordinator (director of a program) or a supervisor (observer or mentor) shares a successful matrix or one-minute paper observed in an SI session informally with the course faculty member, he may find these successful learning strategies incorporated into that faculty member's class the next term.

In their weekly meetings, SI leaders and faculty provide feedback to one another on the most difficult content, why it is difficult, and what strategies will help students better understand it. Faculty appreciate feedback from leaders on the questions and difficulties students are having. Too often they hear such feedback only at the end of the term, when it is too late to make changes for that group of students. SI personnel are trained in processing content, facilitating group work, and developing curriculum. Through conversations with faculty they share these ideas. The most expert faculty realize that they must not only know the content but also know how to make the content understandable to all their students.

Formal Faculty Development. Formal faculty development reviews the role of theory in informing teaching practices. DiPardo and Sperling (2005) argue that expert teachers embrace learning about their teaching; they "tend to regard each new insight as a means toward further inquiry, theory assuming the role of provocateur, stimulating the thinking of all of us who seek to better understand the teaching-learning process and to plot our own context-specific strategies" (p. 138).

As economic pressures on institutions increase and legislators demand more accountability, institutions have begun putting measures in place to improve teaching and learning (Centra, 1982; Eble, 1983; Brookfield, 1990). Attempts to improve teaching include student evaluations (Coleman and McKeachie, 1981), university and grant-funded faculty development projects, workshops, seminars, and formal coursework or advanced degrees.

SI coordinator and supervisor training workshops often include teaching faculty. According to feedback from the trainings, these faculty, who help with the observation and mentoring of leaders, appreciate observing the modeling of learning strategies and practicing them in the simulations (Rosenthal and Bandura, 1978). These trainings help faculty learn new pedagogy, understand active learning and collaboration, and produce good ambassadors on campus for SI.

Increasingly, the International Center for Supplemental Instruction housed at the University of Missouri-Kansas City (UMKC) provides faculty development workshops. These customized workshops review topics such as learning theory, successful learning strategies, conducting qualitative and quantitative research on SI, developing leadership skills in leaders, clinical supervision in SI, negative stereotypes that reduce student achievement (Steele and Aronson, 1995), and assessment and evaluation. In typical faculty development programs, these topics may be discussed but seldom modeled and experienced in depth as they are in SI trainings.

Caffarella and Zinn (1999) and McKeachie (1999) argue for institutional structures that promote faculty development, such as collaboration and collegiality. SI is built on collaboration with faculty in the development of enhanced curriculum, especially in video-based supplemental instruction and interdisciplinary courses. SI supervisors are helpful resources because they are trained in group processing, differentiating important concepts from difficult concepts, and matching learning strategies to content. SI personnel who are integrated into faculty development committees or teaching and learning centers provide valuable expertise to the academy.

Thirty years ago, one could count the number of SI coordinators and supervisors with graduate degrees on one hand. Increasingly, SI programs hire SI staff or provide incentives for them to earn advanced degrees. Such educational credentials not only provide staff with an increased learning base but also provide them with increased credibility in the profession and in regard to the faculty. The University of Missouri-Kansas City has begun a graduate program with SI as a main component to further develop professionals in academic support services.

Benefits to the Administration and to the Institution

Ultimately, administrators and institutions benefit when students learn and when budgets are balanced. SI contributes to both goals.

Student Benefits. When students attend SI regularly, they learn the material more effectively and their grades improve. When students learn more, they tend to stay in the discipline of their choice, reenroll, and persist to graduation. Moreover, they report that they are more satisfied with their courses, even if the faculty do not change their style of teaching the courses. Consistently, research on SI has validated these findings over more than thirty years.

Economic Benefits. The cost to help each student is less than for many traditional support services because SI academic support is not one-on-one. It is helpful for institutional budgets because student retention rates are higher. SI also provides faculty development both indirectly and directly. According to Johnson, Johnson, and Smith (1991), faculty instructional productivity improves when faculty development is integrated into the institution. Participation in SI provides faculty with experiences in collaboration and collegiality, modeling effective learning strategies, and a sense that they can make a difference in the lives of students. According to Brent and Felder (2000) and Boyle and Boice (1998), faculty development that includes mentoring, observation, and supervision greatly decreases the time those faculty need to become effective teachers and full, productive members of the institution. SI provides mentoring for women and minorities, the very faculty who are often marginalized in traditional faculty development programs (Brent and Felder, 2000; Boyle and Boice, 1998).

Overall, SI provides both successful participant faculty development and budget benefits, and it promotes the service component of the institutional mission.

Case Study from South Africa

Currently, higher education in South Africa faces many challenges. The merger of South African Higher Education institutions has brought about a state of flux and uncertainty for staff and students alike. In the midst of this flux, higher education institutions are pressured to widen access, which results in the admission of students who are underprepared for higher education. Simultaneously, the funding formula for government subsidies has been adapted and funding is no longer based on the number of students enrolled, but rather on student retention.

SI as Catalyst for Change. Supplemental Instruction has become a catalyst for change and a vehicle for transformation in South Africa. Students have the opportunity to raise their concerns and needs in sessions, and the SI leaders in turn report these issues to faculty and administrators. This feedback loop has given the students a voice and raised awareness among faculty of the importance of addressing student needs in order to ensure retention.

The University of Port Elizabeth (UPE) embarked on its transformation process in the early 1990s. UPE was originally established under the apartheid system and was mainly oriented toward the needs of the white community. During the transformation process, there was recognition of the need for the transformation of student academic development.

The director of the Centre for Organizational Development (COAD), André Havenga, implemented SI as the catalyst for transformation. According to Wlodkowski and Ginsberg (1995), when students use the principles of peer-facilitated learning (such as SI) in an environment in which they feel safe and respected, they will concentrate and use their imagination and exert more effort in their studies. SI is also cost-effective and has a proven track record. These successes were advocated to students, academic staff, management, and other tertiary institutions in South Africa. In institutions where commitment to the program was lacking, SI was not very successful (Hillman and McCarthy, 1996; Smuts, 1996). The research on SI in South Africa indicated that, because of changing student demographics and needs, the traditional SI model did not always address the needs of students (Clark and Mallon, 1998; Nel and Snow, 2003). Adaptations of the SI program came into existence with the assistance of faculty, SI leaders, and SI supervisors. Through these adaptations, SI grew beyond a mere student academic development program. By taking ownership of the program and becoming involved, the other stakeholders acquired skills associated with SI. Therefore, SI had an impact beyond its traditional role.

At Nelson Mandela Metropolitan University (NMMU) and other South African institutions, lecturers attend SI leader training and SI supervisor training on a regular basis. Feedback from academic staff attending these courses indicates that they have adapted their traditional teaching methods and incorporated SI principles into their lectures, using more interactive lecturing methods, which results in more active student participation in lectures. To further complement this transference of skills, many SI leaders have become lecturers thanks to their involvement with SI and the successful relationships they have built with the academic departments in which they served. To date, thirty-four SI leaders at NMMU have taken up lecturing positions there and at other institutions, mainly as a result of their SI experience. They also bring with them a facilitative style of instruction by incorporating their SI strategy skills into their lectures.

Faculty who have been actively involved in SI have also become involved in other academic development-related areas on campus, including academic orientation, the Post-Graduate Certificate in Higher Education (PGCHE), and other initiatives. Many of these faculty members have conducted research not only in their areas of academic expertise but also in academic development.

Faculty who attend SI training realize the need for feedback. The feedback they receive from their students through questionnaires and from SI leaders in meetings and reports result in academic curricula being adapted to incorporate skills development in the context of the discipline. Combined with the quantitative feedback on SI as provided by the SI supervisor, NMMU identified and created a space for faculty development. In cases where adaptation of the curriculum did not serve the purpose, the SI feedback was used to design a new course or initiative that would better address the needs of the students. SI, thus, was integrated into the curriculum design. "Pockets" of SI skills could be found in the curriculum design, constantly informing and interacting with the academic material. The process did not take place instantly, but sound processes were adhered to. The result was a tried and tested curriculum that addressed the students' needs in ways it could not have done before.

Historically, South African students have been enveloped in a "passive, unquestioning, and conventional milieu" (Vorster and Davies, 1994, p. 168). This results in students having a predominantly external locus of control. The success of SI, however, relies heavily on their active involvement. This results in a new culture of learning in students who have come from this relatively passive learning milieu. It creates a challenging academic experience that forces students to draw on their own resources, rather than external resources. Active student involvement in the learning process has led to greater academic success and higher throughput rates, which in turn has lessened faculty stress.

Six C's of Sustainability. One of the underlying questions for the survival of the SI program in the contested landscape of higher education is its sustainability. Six factors necessary to its sustainability have been identified: namely the "Six C's of Sustainability" (Clark-Unite, 2004).

First, in order for a program to take root and grow, it is imperative that a credible *champion* be appointed to drive the program. The sustainability of the NMMU SI program owes much of its success to the initial leadership of André Havenga, former executive director of COAD.

Contextualizing or *customizing* too is one of the key strategies for sustainability of the SI program. Phrases that come to mind include "adapt or die" and "fitness for purpose." The success of the SI program in South Africa can be attributed to the manner in which it was adapted and molded to fit the divergent contexts of tertiary institutions. However, before the program was endorsed nationally, the program had to be experimented with at the University of Port Elizabeth to ensure its viability for a South African context. After a few years of development, the program became a flagship, and UPE was granted the rights of the National Office. In January 2005 the former University of Port Elizabeth, Port Elizabeth Technikon, and the Port Elizabeth campus of Vista University merged to become the Nelson Mandela Metropolitan University. The SI National Office, which formerly resided at the University of Port Elizabeth, was allowed to continue within the newly formed Nelson Mandela Metropolitan University based on its sound track record. The SI National Office for Southern Africa consists of a head and a deputy head, both of whom are Certified Supplemental Instruction International Trainers and who are responsible for training SI Supervisors in the Southern African region. They are also responsible for ensuring that the quality of the SI model is retained at these institutions. In addition, they facilitate networking between institutions involved in the SI model and they encourage research of the SI model and its effectiveness within the Southern African context.

Central funding is another important factor in sustainability. Without the financial endorsement of the institution, the program is a nonstarter. Financial support demonstrates the institution's commitment to the program. One of the key successes of the NMMU SI program has been that the university has committed itself to the program by providing central funding and underwriting the financial requirements of the SI National Centre (for example, giving release time for the national trainers to conduct supervisor training).

Commitment and buy-in from relevant stakeholders and learners is crucial for the sustainability of the program. Two questions that management frequently ask are, "Does it work?" and "What does it cost?" Havenga's successful "win-win" response to those management questions was another question: "What would it cost the institution if we do not implement the SI program?" The selling point was that SI contributes significantly to improving throughput rates and thereby increases government subsidy.

Capacity building and continuity of staff is another important strategy for sustainability. How do you get the right people onboard? A critical element for the success of the SI program at NMMU has been the emphasis on leadership development and empowerment. Over the years, experienced SI leaders have taken on the roles of assistant supervisors, supervisors, and assistant national trainers. Currently, the NMMU SI campus program is coordinated by a former SI leader who is also a certified national trainer. Accreditation of SI leaders is also being developed in an attempt to provide an incentive, besides financial, to retain SI staff.

Finally, *critical reflection and renewal* is the last important factor. For "reflective practitioners," constant evaluation and renewal is important in order to bring about an improvement in practice: identify the problem, plan the intervention, implement the intervention and evaluate the outcomes, and then use what has been learned to inform the planning, and so the cycle begins again. "Action research" is an important consideration for quality assurance, as outlined by the Higher Education Quality Committee.

Conclusion

To conclude, the benefits of SI at the NMMU have been as follows: ensuring stability during transformation and accommodating the needs of first-generation learners; providing financial incentives in terms of continued enrollment and throughput strategy in response to the government funding formula; and increasing learner satisfaction at the institution with the development of a culture of belonging and the deepening of understanding of what it entails to be studying at a university.

References

Boyer, E. L. *Scholarship Reconsidered: Priorities of the Professoriate.* Princeton, N.J.: Carnegie Foundation for the Advancement of Teaching, 1990.

Boyle, P., and Boice, B. "Systematic Mentoring for New Faculty Teachers and Graduate Teaching Assistants." *Innovative Higher Education,* 1998, 22(3), 157–179.

Brent, R., and Felder, R. M. "Helping New Faculty Get Off to a Good Start." ASEE Annual Conference and Exposition: Engineering, Session 3630: St. Louis, Mo., June 2000. http://www.succeed.ufl.edu/papers/00/00280.pdf. Accessed Aug. 25, 2005.

Brookfield, S. D. *The Skillful Teacher.* San Francisco: Jossey-Bass, 1990.

Caffarella, R. S., and Zinn, L. F. "Professional Development for Faculty: A Conceptual Framework of Barriers and Supports." *Innovative Higher Education,* 1999, 23(4), 241–254.

Camblin, L. D., and Steger, J. A. "Rethinking Faculty Development." *Higher Education,* 2000, 39, 1–18.

Centra, J. A. *Determining Faculty Effectiveness.* San Francisco: Jossey-Bass, 1982.

Clark, C. "Supplemental Instruction for the South African Context: A Case Study at the University of Port Elizabeth." Paper presented at the ACPA/NASPA Convention, Chicago, Mar. 1997.

Clark, C., and Mallon, P. "Supplemental Instruction as a Tool to Improve Student Success at South African Tertiary Institutions." In H. Hudson (ed.), *Proceedings of the South African Association for Academic Development (SAAAD) Conference: 1998.* Bloemfontein, South Africa: University of the Free State, 1998.

Clark-Unite, C. "Supplemental Instruction: A Model for Sustainability in Higher Education." In *Sustaining Education Development Projects.* Port Elizabeth, South Africa: GM South Africa Foundation, 2004.

Coleman, J., and McKeachie, W. J. "Effects of Instructor Course Evaluations on Student Course Selections." *Journal of Educational Psychology*, 1981, 73, 224–226.

DiPardo, A. and Sperling, M. "Theories We Live By." *Research in the Teaching of English*, 2005, 40(2), 137–139.

Eble, K. E. *The Aims of College Teaching*. San Francisco: Jossey-Bass, 1983.

Eleser, C. B., and Chauvin, S. W. "Professional Development How-To's: Strategies for Surveying Faculty Preferences." *Innovative Higher Education*, 1998, 22(3), 181–201.

Hillman J. C., and McCarthy, A. J. "Supplemental Instruction: Facilitating Student Participation in the Learning Process." In J. Vorster (ed.), *Proceedings of the Conference on Student Contributions to Learning: 1996*. Grahamstown, South Africa: Rhodes University, 1996.

Johnson, D. W., Johnson, R. T., and Smith, K. A. *Cooperative Learning: Increasing College Faculty Instructional Productivity*. ASHE-ERIC Report on Higher Education, vol. 91, no. 4. San Francisco: Jossey-Bass, 1991.

Lawler, P. A., and King, K. P. "Refocusing Faculty Development: The View from an Adult Learning Perspective." In T. J. Sork, V. L. Chapman, and R. St. Clair (eds.), *Proceedings of the 41st Annual Adult Education Research Conference: 2000*. Vancouver: University of British Columbia, 2000. www.wsar.wsux.ubcx.ca/aerc/2000/lawlerp&kingk-final.pdf.

McKeachie, W. J. *Teaching Tips: Strategies, Research, and Theory for College and University Teachers*. (10th ed.) Boston: Houghton Mifflin, 1999.

Nel, L., and Snow, B. *Report by the National Centre for Supplemental Instruction Southern Africa at the University of Port Elizabeth for the Department of Academic Development at the University of Missouri-Kansas City: 2003 SI National South African Survey*. Port Elizabeth, South Africa: University of Port Elizabeth, 2003.

Postlethwait, S. "The Events and Philosophy That Started ISETL." Keynote address presented at the annual conference of the International Society for Exploring Teaching and Learning, Cocoa Beach, Fla., Oct. 13–15, 2005.

Rosenthal, T. L., and Bandura, A. "Psychological Modeling: Theory and Practice." In S. L. Garfield and A. E. Bergin (eds.), *Handbook of Psychotherapy and Behavior Change: An Empirical Analysis*. New York: Wiley, 1978.

Skeff, K. M., Stratos, G. A., Mygdal, W., DeWitt, T. A., Manfred, L., Quirk, M., Roberts, K., Greenberg, L., and Bland, C. J. "Faculty Development." *Journal of General Internal Medicine*, 1997, 12(2), 56–63.

Smuts, K. B. "Supplemental Instruction in Law: A Case Study (Focus on the SI Leader)." In J. Vorster (ed.), *Proceedings of the Conference on Student Contributions to Learning: 1996*. Grahamstown, South Africa: Rhodes University, 1996.

Sorrells-Jones, J., and Weaver, D. "Knowledge Workers and Knowledge-Intense Organizations, Part 3: Implications for Preparing Healthcare Professionals." *Journal of Nursing Administration*, 1999, 29(10), 14–21.

Steele, C. M., and Aronson, J. "Stereotype Threat and the Intellectual Test Performance of African-Americans." *Journal of Personality and Social Psychology*, 1995, 69, 797–811.

Vorster, J., and Davies, E. "The SI Leader as a Teaching Resource." Paper presented at the SAAAD annual conference, Durban, South Africa: University of Natal, Dec. 1994.

Weaver, D., and Sorrells-Jones, J. "Knowledge Workers and Knowledge-Intense Organizations, Part 2: Designing and Managing for Productivity." *Journal of Nursing Administration*, 1999, 29(9), 19–25.

Wlodkowski, R. J., and Ginsberg, M. B. *Diversity and Motivation: Culturally Responsive Teaching*. San Francisco: Jossey-Bass, 1995.

SANDRA ZERGER is campus SI coordinator and a certified trainer for the Center for Academic Development and the International Center for Supplemental Instruction at the University of Missouri-Kansas City.

NEW DIRECTIONS FOR TEACHING AND LEARNING • DOI: 10.1002/tl

CATHY CLARK-UNITE *is head, Supplemental Instruction National Office, and a certified SI national trainer at Nelson Mandela Metropolitan University in Port Elizabeth, South Africa.*

LIESL SMITH *is deputy head, Supplemental Instruction National Office, campus SI supervisor, and a certified SI national trainer at Nelson Mandela Metropolitan University in Port Elizabeth, South Africa.*

8

SI can expand past the boundaries of on-campus review sessions. This chapter examines how SI can be implemented in university teaching-learning centers, thematically based learning communities, and online and video-based programs and offers a case study of one such online program.

New Directions for Supplemental Instruction

Sonny L. Painter, Rebecca Bailey, Melinda Gilbert, John Prior

Supplemental Instruction has been effective in increasing students' academic success when used in on-campus review sessions. With increases in technology and academic programs across campuses, it is time to think about expanding outside of those campus boundaries. This chapter explains how SI can be successfully implemented in teaching-learning centers and learning communities, how effective it has been for high school students, and how it could be added to distance learning programs.

SI in Teaching-Learning Centers

Teaching-learning centers at colleges and universities support faculty members by explaining strategies that encourage retention and understanding, not just memorization. These centers often offer faculty workshops and additional materials on how to improve their teaching and implement these important strategies. Teaching-learning centers could become even more helpful by providing workshops or additional resources on the SI strategies that have been proven to increase student retention and understanding.

Constructivist Theory. One of the theories behind the SI model, as well as many teaching-learning models, is Jerome Bruner's constructivist theory (1960). Bruner believes that instructors should work to encourage students to discover principles without the help of the instructor. He

NEW DIRECTIONS FOR TEACHING AND LEARNING, no. 106, Summer 2006   © Wiley Periodicals, Inc.
Published online in Wiley InterScience (www.interscience.wiley.com) • DOI: 10.1002/tl.235

73

strongly encourages instructors to engage the students in active dialogue (that is, Socratic learning). He also believes that the task of the instructor is to evaluate the learner's current state of understanding so that the instructor can then translate the information to be learned into a format that is on the student's current level. One SI strategy that follows this theory is redirecting student questions. Instead of the instructor stepping in to answer students' questions, he or she asks the class if anyone else knows the answer. Students process information differently when the information comes from a peer. Wait time is also important; it is the time that elapses between question and answer during which the student can think about the question and where he or she can find the answer individually. Another Socratic learning strategy is reciprocal questioning, an alternating question-and-answer process that aids students in a deeper understanding of content. The professor allows the student to ask a question first, and then the professor asks a question of the student. Another SI strategy that follows Socratic theory is concept mapping. A concept map is a web diagram to help explore knowledge, brainstorm ideas, and organize large amounts of material. This can help translate information into a format that is easier for the students to understand (University of Missouri-Kansas City, 2004).

FCL Model: Fostering a Community of Learners. Another learning model used in teaching-learning centers is Fostering a Community of Learners (FCL). FCL is a popular teaching-learning program that was created by Joe Campione and Ann Brown at Stanford University in 1996 (Shulman and Shulman, 2004). It helps teachers learn how to "teach for understanding." FCL teachers use a family of pedagogical approaches designed to help students become "reasoners" and sense-makers in various content domains. There are four FCL principles of learning: activity, reflection, collaboration, and community. One of the main ideas behind FCL is to break down large topics and then recombine them during discussion into interlocking subtopics that can be studied by subgroups of students and then presented to other students (Schoenfeld, 2004). "FCL teachers look at teaching as a process rather than telling, and of learning as a process rather than repeating or restating" (Shulman and Shulman, 2004, p. 261).

The FCL model embodies many of the characteristics of Supplemental Instruction. Supplemental Instruction uses strategies that help students not just to memorize and regurgitate information but to understand and retain it for future courses. Many of the SI strategies (such as concept mapping, small group discussions, and so on) break down larger topics into smaller concepts that are easier to understand; once those smaller concepts are understood, they are put back together so students can understand the whole. SI leaders interact with students in sessions and redirect questions back to the student or to other students in the session instead of using the normal lecture format, in which the professor simply speaks to the class and answers students' questions.

Because of the philosophical similarities between FCL and SI, integrating the two makes sense. SI theoretically uses the same four principles as FCL: SI uses varying activities to engage students in their own learning process, the regular use of wait time in SI sessions gives students opportunities to reflect on current material, students collaborate in SI sessions to come up with answers to their own questions, and SI fosters a community for students in and outside of the classroom. If teachers in the FCL model and other teaching-learning models were taught the many SI strategies to use in the classroom and had SI available for their individual classes, their students would have higher GPA's, higher graduation rates, and lower DWF rates.

SI in Learning Communities

Recent research on innovative approaches to teaching has turned the attention of administrators and faculty to the concept of learning communities. Learning communities are an approach to curriculum design that coordinates two or more courses into a single program of instruction. There are three main ways to design a learning community: content courses focused on one common theme, skill courses combined with a content course, and integrated general studies courses for occupational programs (Rasmussen and Skinner, 1997). Each learning community, regardless of design, is usually paired with a seminar course facilitated by a faculty or staff member. The seminar course serves to tie the two main courses together and enhances the students' learning in their courses by helping them see the commonalities across the subject areas.

Whether residential or nonresidential, learning communities help students build a sense of community and support on campus, in turn leading to greater retention and academic achievement among these students. The educational experiences of students involved in learning communities are more meaningful, because they learn to think critically across disciplines. The community aspect of the model affords students the opportunity to learn and problem-solve in a collaborative environment. Students benefit from the learning community model academically, personally, socially, and professionally.

The integrated approach used by learning communities is believed to be more compatible with the way people naturally learn and more relevant to the real world. Because Supplemental Instruction was designed to give students the opportunity to interact as they construct knowledge, SI and learning communities would seem to be a natural partnership. The overall goals and objectives of Supplemental Instruction and learning communities are similar for both students and faculty members.

Students in learning communities have a higher level of collaboration with their classmates and spend more time on course material than students who are not in learning communities, because it is natural for the former students to create study groups and work together on projects. Collaboration with classmates and spending more time on task with course materials are two objectives of Supplemental Instruction. Another similarity between LCs and SI is the peer educator component. Learning communities employ a peer educator who has participated in the program previously and taken the courses associated with the learning community. Outside of the classroom, the peer educators assist students with the content of the courses as well as issues such as study skills, learning strategies, and time management. Peer educators are similar to SI leaders in that both have previously taken and succeeded in the course and both work to assist students with the course material. In order to better serve learning communities, peer educators could be trained as SI leaders. The peer educators–SI leaders would thus be better equipped in teaching and demonstrating learning strategies and techniques to students, but most importantly, they would be better equipped to assist the students in becoming independent learners. The students who participate in learning communities would become lifelong learners, able to think critically across disciplines and not needing to rely on being taught the information.

When Supplemental Instruction is integrated into learning communities it benefits the faculty members involved as well as the students. Learning communities are designed to create higher levels of faculty interaction with the students than is traditionally the case. The same is true for courses supported by Supplemental Instruction. By working closely with the faculty members, students are able to increase their knowledge of the subject matter and are encouraged to explore the topics of the course in more depth than they would do otherwise. In this type of setting, faculty members are able to form closer relationships with students and more likely to serve as mentors. Students demonstrate the benefits of gaining this depth of knowledge of the subject matter and relationships with the faculty by earning higher grades than those who are not involved in learning communities or Supplemental Instruction.

SI in Online Learning Communities

With the increase in the availability of technology, colleges are able to offer distance-learning courses via the Internet. Classes formed online can be looked at as learning communities in themselves. In an online learning community, students, instructors, and peer educators communicate via e-mail, discussion boards, and instant messaging. Interaction in online learning communities, as in traditional learning communities, is a combination of instructor-student, peer educator–student, and student-student communication. In this environment, students spend more time communicating with and educating each other than they do in a traditional learning environment. Peer educators in online learning communities facilitate discussions on the course content and serve as a resource for students. One drawback to this model is that students can read what other students have written without participating themselves. However, with a peer educator facilitating the discussion, students are more likely to become involved.

NEW DIRECTIONS FOR TEACHING AND LEARNING • DOI: 10.1002/tl

The online learning community model is similar in structure to the traditional SI model. Having peer educators trained as SI leaders, and having the instructors trained on the SI model, would only serve to enhance the online learning community. Although there is great potential in serving students through online learning communities, they still pose unique challenges, as will be discussed later in the chapter.

VSI in High Schools

SI continues to reach more populations. As discussed in Chapter Five, the SI pedagogy has been transformed to fit the classroom, evolving into what has been named Video-based Supplemental Instruction, or VSI (University of Missouri-Kansas City, 2005). Through VSI, students can control the pace of the information by stopping the video lecture and applying SI techniques to understand and retain new information. Because the content is delivered by a professor on video and the class is supervised by a trained facilitator, these modified college courses can be introduced to new populations such as underprepared college students (as seen in Chapter Five) and underserved high school students in rural areas.

Dual-Credit Courses. Many high schools are now offering dual-credit courses in their curriculum (Finken, 2003). Students complete high school coursework as well as gain college credit by enrolling in courses that meet the requirements of both educational systems. As society's demand for a college education increases, so do requests for these courses to be offered in high schools. However, many high school teachers are not qualified to teach dual-credit courses. This is especially true in rural high schools where teachers lack the convenience of a nearby university or college where they might take classes to meet the requirements. Rural high schools have to look to distance education programs to meet the demands for dual-credit courses. This is where SI (through VSI) can meet the needs of high school students.

Because VSI courses require only a trained facilitator, many high schools can implement this dual-credit, distance education program directly into their curriculum using teachers who lack the qualifications to teach the requested college courses. However, a teacher must go through a two-day training not only to understand the policies and procedure for administrating the dual-credit course but also to gain valuable training in facilitating the learning in the classroom (University of Missouri-Kansas City, 2005). After training, teachers are able to employ many of the proven learning strategies used in SI, such as checking for understanding, developing a collaborative learning environment, redirecting questions, and using wait time. Trained facilitators can easily implement VSI courses into their individual high school's established curricula.

Benefits of Implementing VSI. VSI courses bring many benefits that other distance education, dual-credit courses do not offer. One of the most attractive features of a VSI course is its asynchronous delivery of content. Many distance education courses require schools to structure schedules around specific broadcast times. VSI courses allow teachers to integrate the course into the school's existing course schedule and offer flexibility for unique or unforeseen events such as pep rallies, parent-teacher conferences, and snow days. High school VSI courses have been designed to accommodate these types of events and to be completed in the longer academic school year versus the traditional sixteen-week college semester.

Asynchronous delivery also allows for processing of new content. Students can stop the video, ask questions, and understand the material before moving on to more new content. This allows them to process smaller pieces of information instead of handling a mass of lecture material. They can also replay the videos to review specific content for clarity. Finally, video lectures accommodate students who are absent from class by allowing them to watch missed lectures on their own time.

Another benefit of the VSI course is its consistency. For example, a traditional dual-credit course, Western Civilization, could be taught and evaluated by many different individual high school teachers for a particular college or university. However, the VSI Western Civilization course is taught and evaluated by a single video professor, providing greater consistency of content and evaluation for all students taking the course.

Above all, VSI benefits high schools by bringing the SI model to the high school students and teachers. In the SI model, the teacher-facilitator's focus changes from delivery of content to student-centered learning, allowing students the time and attention needed to process, understand, and retain the content. Teachers are removed from the position of lecturer in the VSI course and now serve "as the model student, demonstrating how to think about and learn the material of the discipline" (University of Missouri-Kansas City, 2005, p. 8). In this way, SI meets the needs of high school students through VSI courses, making them better prepared for college.

SI and Technology

Technology has changed the face of education. Trends show that colleges and universities will have to turn to technology to meet the needs of the increasing numbers of students pursuing a higher education degree (Lorenzetti, 2003). The solution: online courses. Online courses offer many benefits, including flexibility of time and location (Romeo, 2001). As more and more courses are being offered online and students are electing to take these courses to fit into their demanding schedules, SI has to modify to support these virtual learners.

In online courses, as in traditional classrooms, there exists a population of students who need additional help in processing content. Effective SI sessions have characteristics that allow students to process information efficiently. These characteristics include a live (synchronous) environment, student-to-

NEW DIRECTIONS FOR TEACHING AND LEARNING • DOI: 10.1002/tl

leader interactions, and student-to-student interactions (Painter, 2004). A live environment permits sessions to be on-pace with the supported course and addresses the needs of the students immediately. Student-to-leader interactions allow for leaders to check for understanding and allot sufficient processing time and let students communicate with an expert on the subject to get their questions answered. Student-to-student interactions are necessary to allow students to find additional resources for answers (other students), increase understanding of materials by processing and struggling with new materials, and allow the leader to check for understanding by observing the communication among students. These characteristics must be present in order for SI sessions to be effective and must be incorporated into online SI sessions.

Advantages to Online Sessions. There are many advantages to offering online SI sessions for a course (Painter, 2004). Online sessions can be held anywhere and at any time. SI leaders can easily redirect questions as they do in traditional SI sessions. They can facilitate discussions and conversations, which helps control dominating students and confrontations. There is less presentation anxiety for students, because they are not in front of a class. Additional resources can be easily accessed and distributed to students using online formats. The leader can set up online quizzes and surveys to quickly check for understanding, which can also provide immediate feedback of results to students, often better than in traditional sessions. Leaders can easily track attendance of students through communication software. Sessions can be recorded and used as additional resources for students who have missed any sessions or choose to review past sessions.

Disadvantages to Online Sessions. Along with the advantages of online SI sessions come disadvantages, however (Painter, 2004). These disadvantages can be looked at from basically two perspectives: the providers and the users of the online SI sessions.

One of the main disadvantages for providers is the cost of the technology to support the session. The cost of the software, hardware, and technical support needed to administer an effective online SI session can be restrictive for some student support programs in today's higher education institutions, which face rising costs everywhere. In addition, many software products limit the number of users at one time, which restricts the number of students who can be served. In cases where there is no limit to the number of students who can participate in an online session, SI leaders may have more difficulties managing multiple students than in a traditional SI session setting. Once students are in the online session, maintaining their attention is also difficult because online discussions and interactions tend to be slower and students can easily jump into and out of the discussions, losing their focus on the topic. Also, communication online is somewhat complicated because many math and chemistry symbols are hard to use or are not readily supported with today's technology.

From the user's perspective, a big issue is technical problems. The SI leader's software and hardware may be adequate, but the students may not have the proper software or hardware or compatibility to participate in the online sessions. For example, students' computers may not have the cameras and microphones necessary for discussions or may have an operating system that is not supported by the software. They may also have additional software that prevents the communication software from running correctly, such as pop-up blockers and firewalls. In addition, the Internet connection may be so slow that communication among students and leaders becomes ineffective. All these disadvantages must be considered and remedied before considering hosting online SI sessions. Continuing advances in technologies are overcoming these obstacles daily.

Using a Variety of Technologies. To implement online SI sessions, one must consider the variety of technologies available to communicate online. As stated earlier, in order for online SI sessions to be effective they must be live (Painter, 2004). Thus, SI sessions must use synchronous technologies. Some synchronous technologies include text chat, electronic whiteboards, video- and audioconferencing, application sharing, and polling (Shepherd, 2000).

Shepherd (2000) states, "Text chat is the most basic of synchronous methods and the easiest to implement." Electronic whiteboards allow students to have "a common visual working space." Students draw, type, or insert images on the same whiteboard, allowing for a collaborative work area. Audio- and videoconferencing provide real-time discussions among the online students. Application-sharing features of many communication software programs allow students to jointly view and work on the same documents at the same time. Real-time polling is an additional feature that allows SI leaders and students to get immediate feedback during online sessions. All of these technologies are live (synchronous) and promote student-to-leader and student-to-student interactions, thus creating an effective online learning environment.

Providing accessible support for the new generation of virtual learners is very possible. Advancements in technology are continually eliminating many of the barriers preventing institutional and student use of online learning environments. As these barriers break down, an adapted SI model must be in place to provide effective student support.

Case Study: Oxford Brookes University

PAL (Peer Assisted Learning) was introduced at the Business School at Oxford Brookes University in the early 1990s (it was originally known as Supplemental Instruction). Volunteer second- and third-year students—PAL leaders—run sessions for students on core modules. In recruiting PAL leaders, we look for academically strong students with outgoing personalities. They are trained in facilitation skills and supported throughout the year by a member of the staff. PAL sessions run once a week for each of the modules and give students an opportunity to improve their understanding and solve problems. They last for an hour and are informal "drop-in" sessions.

New Directions for Teaching and Learning • DOI: 10.1002/tl

The philosophy of PAL is that the PAL leaders do not teach; they facilitate. They act as a catalyst for the group, encouraging all members to participate in sharing their knowledge and experiences. In successful PAL sessions all the students gain from learning together, including the PAL leaders themselves, who develop important interpersonal skills that can be of real benefit to them in their future careers.

The PAL program proved very successful and is now offered to over two thousand students across the school. However, by 2004 it was noticeable that, although the number of volunteers for PAL leadership had remained steady, their commitment declined during the course of a year. Generally, eight to ten PAL leaders were recruited each year but by the end of the year only three or four of the most dedicated remained active. We were aware of the increasing pressures on students as they juggled their studies, paid work, and social life, and PAL leaders were no exception to this. Participants were also asking for more flexibility in the availability of PAL sessions, while at the same time the PAL leaders were having more difficulty finding the time to devote to the sessions.

PAL Online. The development of PAL Online (using the Web CT virtual learning environment) sought to reconcile these conflicting pressures and to provide a facility that would not only give both PAL leaders and participants greater flexibility but also increase the usage of PAL.

The PAL Online trial was used on two first-year modules.

Introductory Model. The first was a small (220 students) introductory module. A Web CT site was set up solely for PAL Online and designed to support exam review. Ninety of the students on the module made a total of 2,194 visits to the site—an average of 24 visits per student. Some valuable discussions resulted, with students sharing their knowledge, facilitated by the PAL leaders.

Although they appear impressive, the statistics for visits to the site can be misleading—of the ninety students who visited the site only ten posted messages. The other eighty students visited the site, looked through the messages, but did not make a posting themselves. Participants who read the messages without contributing themselves are known as *lurkers* (or less pejoratively, as *browsers*). This is a well-known and much-discussed phenomenon (Salmon, 2000), and the key to a successful online discussion is to turn lurkers into contributors.

Student Evaluation. Student evaluation was positive. Students welcomed the opportunity to share their knowledge and sources of information, but it was pointed out that the involvement of more students in the discussion was needed. Students obviously appreciated the flexibility offered online, compared to the weekly meetings. One night there was some quite lively and relevant discussion at 1:30 A.M.!

Large Core Module. Following the positive reaction to the first trial, PAL Online was introduced to a large core module. With over six hundred students on the module there was some concern that the site might become swamped with messages and the PAL leaders would be unable to cope. This notion proved to be rather optimistic. As with the first trial the site was visited frequently. Over four hundred students visited the site, making a total of eighty-four hundred visits. However, of the four hundred students only eleven posted messages and the exchange of knowledge was minimal. The fact that the students on this module were all experienced users of Web CT (especially compared to the students in the first trial) made this lack of activity even more surprising. There was, however, one important difference between this and the first trial. There was one particularly good PAL leader, very active in the first trial who, due to pressure of work, was hardly involved in the second trial. Salmon (2000) points out that the seeding of the discussion by e-moderators taking an active role is a crucial factor in encouraging online participation.

Conclusions from the Trials. The trials showed that there is a high level of interest in PAL Online. The results of the second trial indicate that good PAL leaders are just as important online as face-to-face. Both trials had a large number of lurkers, but even if they do not contribute, these students gain from the knowledge being exchanged in the discussions. In fact, if the lurkers are taken into account, PAL Online reached a far greater percentage of the student cohort than face-to-face PAL.

There is, however, one negative aspect to set against these positive results, and that is the issue of the accuracy of postings. One answer posted by a student in response to a question from another student was incorrect. The PAL leaders did not pick up on this, and although a later posting from another student gave the correct answer, he did not refer to the incorrect answer. An erroneous statement in a face-to-face PAL session will be heard by a maximum of ten students. In contrast, the online posting could have been read by all four hundred students who visited the site. The introduction to the site emphasizes that teaching staff are not involved. However, academics do have an overall responsibility for the learning on a module and PAL Online is part of this.

In sum, the trials showed that PAL Online has potential, but for it to be realized PAL leaders will have to take more time-consuming and responsible roles. Our experience in working with teams of PAL leaders has shown that they have the necessary skills and dedication. Greater involvement from the PAL leaders would combine two powerful forms of learning—online learning and peer-supported learning—and make a significant contribution to the existing online learning environment.

Key Points in the Further Development of PAL Online. There are several key points to consider in continuing to develop PAL Online:

- *Recruit and train PAL Online leaders.* The trials have shown that some leaders are more effective online than others. Recruitment and training of a dedicated PAL Online team would attract students who are particularly interested in working online.

- *Turn lurkers into contributors.* The trials attracted a high percentage of students (40 percent on the first trial and 65 percent on the second) but only a very small percentage actually joined in the discussion. This is disheartening for the PAL leaders and disappointing for the students who do not receive a reply to their postings. Salmon (2000) makes the point that both participants and e-moderators need training in learning online. The transcripts from the trials can be used to demonstrate the discussion process and how students can benefit from taking part in the discussion.
- *Maintain student interest in the site.* If students are to be encouraged to use the site regularly, they need to find new information or postings whenever they visit the site. Increasing the number of discussion postings will provide some of this interest. The regular posting of messages by PAL leaders—suggesting topics for discussion, review questions, and so on— is also important.
- *Deal with the pressures on PAL Online leaders.* E-moderating is a time-consuming process. If student participation is to be encouraged and maintained, the site needs to be checked daily. If checking for incorrect postings is added to their tasks, that may be too much to expect from PAL leaders, who are, after all, volunteers. Against this, the trials have shown that, by facilitating online discussion, the PAL leaders have the potential to make a significant contribution to learning. PAL leaders are well qualified to take on the task, and if they were paid (and could avoid taking on unskilled work off campus), they would be playing a useful role in the learning process, from which they themselves would gain valuable skills.

Conclusion

As this chapter has shown, there are many reasons why Supplemental Instruction should be expanded beyond campus boundaries. SI has already been effective in so many areas that it makes sense to implement it in new areas. Because teaching-learning communities and learning communities embody many of the same theories and philosophies as SI, it seems only natural to integrate the two. Using technology to deliver SI to students can be an effective way to stay up-to-date with the growing demands of students' busy schedules and distance learning. However, there are many things to take into consideration as this is more thoroughly developed. As evidenced in the case study, the SI leaders must be active participants in the online model in order to maximize student participation. Furthermore, because it is difficult to deliver all SI techniques through the online model, both the leaders and instructors should be well trained on SI techniques, and training should be modified to address the issues unique to online communities. After further research and development, online SI sessions could be a viable option in the future. Where people gather physically or virtually to learn, SI can be there.

References

Bruner, J. *The Process of Education.* Cambridge, Mass.: Harvard University Press, 1960.

Finken, D. "Double Duty." *Community College Week,* 2003, *16*(4), 6–8.

Lorenzetti, J. "Thirty-Two Distance Education Trends." *Distance Education Report,* 2003, *7*(21), 1–2, 6.

Painter, S. L. "Online SI: To Boldly Go Where No SI Has Gone Before." Presentation at the Third International Conference on Supplemental Instruction, Boston, June 2004.

Rasmussen, G., and Skinner, E. "An Overview of Learning Communities." *Learning Communities: Getting Started.* Maricopa Community College, Tempe, and Gate Way Community College, Phoenix, 1997.

Romeo, L. "Asynchronous Environment for Teaching and Learning: Literacy Trends and Issues Online." *Delta Kappa Gamma Bulletin,* 2001, *67*(3), 24–28.

Salmon, G. "E-Moderating: The Key to Teaching and Learning Online." Paper presented at the BEST Conference, Edinburgh, 2000.

Schoenfeld, A. "Multiple Learning Communities: Students, Teachers, Instructional Designers, and Researchers." *Journal of Curriculum Studies,* 2004, *36*(2), 237–255.

Shepherd, C. *The Real-Time Online Tutor,* 2000. http://www.fastrak-consulting.co.uk/tactix/features/realtime/realtime.htm. Accessed June 22, 2005.

Shulman, L., and Shulman, J. "How and What Teachers Learn: A Shifting Perspective." *Journal of Curriculum Studies,* 2004, *36*(2), 257–271.

University of Missouri-Kansas City. *Supplemental Instruction Leader Resource Manual.* Kansas City: Curators of the University of Missouri, 2004.

University of Missouri-Kansas City. *The VSI High School Dual-Credit Program Facilitator's Manual.* Kansas City: Curators of the University of Missouri, 2005.

SONNY L. PAINTER *is the coordinator of the Dual-Enrollment High School Video-based Supplemental Instruction Program in the Center for Academic Development at the University of Missouri-Kansas City.*

REBECCA BAILEY *is the program coordinator for the coaching program in the Center for Academic Development at the University of Missouri-Kansas City.*

MELINDA GILBERT *is a student in the master's of counseling and guidance program and is a graduate intern at the Center for Academic Development at University of Missouri-Kansas City.*

JOHN PRIOR *is a senior lecturer in management at the Business School of Oxford Brookes University, Oxford, UK.*

NEW DIRECTIONS FOR TEACHING AND LEARNING • DOI: 10.1002/tl

*A permutation of the original program, TeamSI represents
an ambitious attempt to improve both students' deep
understanding of their knowledge in a professional discipline and their self-development as more mature learners
and leaders.*

TeamSI: A Resource for Integrating and Improving Learning

Carin Muhr, Deanna C. Martin

Medical faculties recognize it as problematic that many students retain little of their basic science knowledge by the time they enter their clinical
studies. The problem is exacerbated by the fact that many students, eager
to begin treating patients, lack enthusiasm for their basic science studies.
They fail to see the essential connection this coursework has with the practice of medicine. The authors observed that a more structured and sophisticated form of Supplemental Instruction might afford students the
opportunity to connect the principles of the basic sciences with their clinical practice.

Teamsi, an adaptation of SI that addresses this problem, is designed to
improve the quality of medical education by deepening the integrated
knowledge base of medical students and improving both their communication and their leadership skills (Blanc and Martin, 1994). The student members of the first application of TeamSI are medical students from the
third-semester neurobiology course and students from the ninth-semester
clinical neurology course. Experienced SI leaders, themselves advanced

We wish to thank the Swedish Council for Higher Education for its generous financial
support that made this project possible; all the TeamSI leaders for their great enthusiasm and never ending creativity, hard work, and never failing support; Dr. Robert Blanc
for generously sharing his wisdom; our colleague Professor Aldskogius for his kind and
very valuable support throughout the project; personal development consultant Martin
Pollak for his inspiring collaboration; and all the SI students who were willing to join
the project and help with valuable feedback and the development of TeamSI.

students, were chosen to facilitate the student groups. Completing the team were participating faculty from the courses, the project director, a neurologist certified in both neuroscience and clinical neurology, and the project collaborator, Deanna Martin, who was the founder of SI.

The SI Students

The project director and the TeamSI leaders presented TeamSI to the students at the start of their courses: Neurobiology Block (NBB), a basic neuroscience course, and Clinical Neurology (CN), respectively. Voluntary participants included 104 students (sixty-six women and thirty-eight men) of which 60 students (thirty-six women, twenty-four men) were third-semester (NBB) and 44 (thirty women, fourteen men) were ninth-semester students (CN). In total, volunteers represented 42 percent of those in the NBB course and 34 percent of those in the CN course. The representation of women participating was slightly greater than their representation in the classes.

The SI Groups

The SI groups were formed with about equal numbers of students, both women and men, from each of the two courses. The students had eight to ten SI meetings, each scheduled for two hours, during the five-week period of the NBB course. The SI students decided together with their SI leader when they wanted to meet. The CN course continued beyond the end of the NBB course, and the students from clinical neurology were offered two final meetings for exam preparation.

The SI Leaders

The SI leaders chosen for TeamSI, with one exception, had prior experience working in the SI program at the School of Medicine. A total of twelve SI leaders—five females and seven males—received training for TeamSI. Five of the six TeamSI leaders graduated from medical school after working one semester; one continued and five more were trained for TeamSI. All the TeamSI leaders were in their last year of medical school, their tenth and eleventh semesters. In addition, all had worked as medical doctors for limited periods of time.

TeamSI Leader Training

As is traditional in SI, the TeamSI leaders were trained to listen carefully to questions from the SI participants. They were instructed not to answer any questions directly but to redirect these questions to the students who would themselves, in the collective interaction of the group, search for the answers. As usual, the students were permitted to consult textbooks and lecture notes. The SI leader had the responsibility to see that all SI participants

NEW DIRECTIONS FOR TEACHING AND LEARNING • DOI: 10.1002/tl

had their questions considered by the group. The leader also made sure that the discussion was constructive, that it moved forward, that important issues were covered, and that each student achieved understanding of the content. Experienced in the training of SI leaders, the project director (who is also the campus SI supervisor) recognized that the design of TeamSI required more of its leaders than in the traditional SI program, and accordingly, lengthened the training period from two to three days. This further training focused on collaborating in a team and also on handling students from two different levels in the same SI group.

In TeamSI, the leaders were expected to have a firm grasp on both the basic science principles and the clinical applications of those principles. The leader would lead the group indirectly to discover the clinical relevance of the basic concept or the reverse, the basic concept underlying clinical practice. In addition, ongoing training was provided on a weekly basis. In training, the role of the TeamSI leaders was strengthened and systematically developed by using "critical friends" (Costa and Kallick, 1993) and special activities to deepen self-reflection.

An additional goal for the project director was to enhance the leaders' personal development in order to improve their leadership skills. Therefore, weekly supervisory sessions of sixty to ninety minutes took place. The supervisory session followed the format of a regular SI meeting. All SI leaders reported what had taken place in their individual SI meetings and what each wanted to raise for further discussion. The project director, as trainer, focused attention on the communication among the students from the different semesters and the learning climate generated in the group. Problems were raised and solutions offered by members of the group, who often based their remarks on their own similar experiences. Sometimes these suggestions were tried out in role playing. At the next supervisory session, a follow-up of each problem was reported. The supervisory sessions concluded with a written reflection by each SI leader on what she or he had learned, and these comments were collected. The attendance during the sessions was very satisfactory.

The TeamSI leaders were invited to participate in a five-day retreat designed to enhance their ability to cope with stress. The retreat focused on TeamSI leaders' responses to the stress of leading collaborative learning groups. Meditation, massage, discussion, and reflection supplemented lectures delivered by experts in the field of stress reduction. All TeamSI leaders elected to participate.

In order to provide the leaders with training in how to identify and use creative remedies to conflict, the project director, in collaboration with an external personal development consultant, arranged a series of seminars that all of the leaders attended. The content of these seminars relied on the work of Kay Pollak (1998). One of the basic premises is that everyone always has a choice among reactions to what is happening. Building habits of action and reaction creates our own reality, our own world. In SI terms, every student in the SI group is both a valuable tutor and a learner, as is everyone on the SI team. The discussion extended to include every patient that the students would meet in their professional lives. A great deal of fruitful discussion ensued about choosing one's reactions to events and encounters.

Structure and Method of the TeamSI Program

In the SI groups students were initially assigned to sit with members of their own class. They soon, however, asked for a change as they saw the value in pairing with students who were not at their same academic level. During the SI sessions, different modes of collaborative learning were used to accommodate the varied concepts and data sets presented in the cases. Pairs of students undertook to explicate preassigned segments of the case under consideration. The pairs used appropriate resource materials and dictionaries available in the meeting room for their "look-ups" (subtopics from the case that required research). The pairs devoted time to designing diagrams, graphs, and other types of visual and linguistic aids for use in their presentations. After each presentation, the other students in the group offered critiques, asked questions, and made comments as they sought to bring resolution to a complicated clinical problem.

The TeamSI leaders were responsible for designing the case studies. In a given week, all TeamSI groups analyzed the same case problem. The case problems were discussed and approved by the project director and the faculty. The case studies of major neurological disorders contained embedded factors that required students to understand in depth both the neurological problems and the associated basic science principles.

TeamSI developed a formalized structure wherein the leaders, the project director, and professors worked together. The project design also included the use of SI supervision to synchronize and enhance the effectiveness of the groups as well as questionnaires, and as already noted, "critical friends." Critical friends is a widely recognized method in which one colleague observes another colleague. The "friends" then analyze the interaction among the students as well as between the leader and the students. In TeamSI, after this observation the leader, the "friends," and the project director met to discuss what they learned. Summary observations were shared during supervisory sessions with all the TeamSI leaders. The purposes of these sessions were several: to improve the quality of the case-based discussions, to improve the leadership skills of the TeamSI leaders, with special focus on the creative handling and resolution of conflicts that arise in group settings, and to develop a training plan for subsequent terms. In all respects, these sessions helped foster a collegial relationship on TeamSI. Being involved as professionals in this relationship was judged most important to the personal development of the TeamSI leaders.

Previous experience with SI has shown that the SI leaders will, through their contact with the students in the SI groups, learn what the students do (and more importantly, do not) comprehend of the content of lectures and seminars. Students in the class will usually not reveal their lack of understanding to the professors, who are the persons evaluating them. To build a bridge between students and faculty, we invited the faculty to take part in the TeamSI meetings. No personal information about students was conveyed in these sessions. Instead, the meetings focused on which content areas were the most problematic.

Results and Evaluation

Evaluation of TeamSI took several forms.

TeamSI Students. Focus groups of students were interviewed by external pedagogues from the Unit for Development of Pedagogy and Interactive Learning (UPI) at Uppsala University. Typical NBB student statements emerging from these interviews resembled these: "It was very valuable to gain insight into the clinical side. It was easier to reach understanding and realize what is important." "We started to study earlier than otherwise. We rehearsed areas which we would not have done on our own." The students expressed appreciation that the SI sessions focused on cases and not simply on the questions that might be expected on the exams.

Evaluators cited a typical response from a student in the CN class: "We learned what we really wanted to understand and to know. I was positively surprised . . . because it [what we were discussing] was well based on the reality in which we will live. " Evaluators also reported as typical the remark of a female student from the same class: "We learn important and valuable things . . . those things which I have always wondered about, but never got to look into."

TeamSI Leaders. Focus groups and interviews with the TeamSI leaders, conducted by the project collaborator and the project director, revealed a clear interest in pedagogy. They observed that the project had piqued their interest both concerning the courses in which they served as SI leaders and the courses they attended themselves. They realized that much instruction could be improved, and further, how it might be improved. They expressed willingness to share these experiences with the faculty, and they took on responsibility to help with the improvement. The TeamSI leaders in their final term of medical studies also noted how clear it became to them that students themselves have the greatest responsibility for their own learning.

In interviews, several TeamSI leaders noted that they valued their experience for the ways in which they were able to enrich other students' lives both personally and academically. They also claimed to have developed insight into their own behavior as it was reflected in the group process. One of the TeamSI leaders noted that he had joined the SI team in hopes of becoming a better leader. He offered that he had always been at the top of his class and he wanted to work on his leadership skills. He also expressed a common theme: "[In SI] . . . we are constantly reflecting on our experiences."

All the TeamSI leaders placed great value on the seminars devoted to creating remedies to conflict. They found that these had a significant impact on their encounters with other persons in their everyday lives. They became more aware of their emotions, and knowing there was a choice, were better able to take control over their reactions. They recognized the challenge in handling difficult situations and saw those as opportunities for effective leadership and personal growth. Furthermore, the critical friends procedure was seen as very valuable in helping them stay focused on the way their own attitudes and behavior affected the group. They became willing to look at their own behavior with the group before making judgments about the students. The TeamSI leaders valued these insights about themselves more than any other part of the leadership and self-development training.

The SI leaders greatly improved and deepened their understanding of the subject matter in neurobiology and clinical neurology. In particular, they realized the importance of basic science as a ground for the clinics. They had not seen this as clearly at the time of their own studies and expressed satisfaction at sharing this insight with the younger students.

TeamSI Professor. The professor in charge of neurobiology was interviewed. He expressed his enthusiasm for the TeamSI project. He provided each SI leader with the latest edition of a textbook in neurobiology, handouts, and other important study material for his course. He also expressed the view that integrating students from neurobiology and clinical neurology courses is very valuable. He noted that clinical neurology is the obvious application of functional neurobiology. In practice, it is essential to understand directly the interaction between function and structure, which forms the base for diagnosing almost all neurological diseases. Furthermore, he stated it is the essential background for the following: choosing the best available treatment, understanding the function of this treatment, and establishing a prognosis for the patient. He expressed awareness that the students from NBB asked for clinical applications while the more advanced students from CN considered it important to rehearse what they had learned earlier, thereby reflecting on prior knowledge as they internalized their clinical teachings.

Concerning interactions with TeamSI leaders, the professor expressed satisfaction with their time together. He noted how easily they accepted responsibilities, how focused they were on the subjects, how interested they were in their leadership role, and how highly skilled they seemed to be in leading groups. He reported several contacts with the TeamSI leaders both in groups and individually. During the project, he had expressed his willingness to help the TeamSI leaders in their own mastery of the subject matter. The professor finally expressed an interest in continued contact. He especially wanted feedback from the TeamSI leaders on the NBB course itself: what students found difficult to understand, what they expressed about the course as a whole, and what opinions and suggestions the TeamSI leaders had about NBB. In summary, the professor's experiences were very positive and he would gladly continue his collaboration with the SI program.

NEW DIRECTIONS FOR TEACHING AND LEARNING • DOI: 10.1002/tl

TeamSI Leaders as Physicians. The TeamSI leaders were brought together for a follow-up evaluation of their experience of what TeamSI had contributed to their professional lives. Now practicing physicians, they generalized that SI had helped them be more successful professionals. They again agreed, when reflecting back on their role as SI leaders and the training they received, that having increased their insight into their own behavior was the single most valuable outcome for them. They found this valuable in their daily work as physicians, both when dealing with patients and when collaborating with colleagues.

One of the SI leaders who worked as an SI leader for four years and as a medical doctor for one year prefaced his answer by noting that the term *doctor* derives from the Latin term *docere* meaning *to teach* and stated that he had learned more from SI concerning handling different and sometimes difficult situations with patients and colleagues than in all his regular medical training. Another SI leader, who had worked as a medical doctor for two years, said this: "Everything I do as a doctor somehow involves teaching, so TeamSI has for me been very rewarding." They also expressed the existential view that TeamSI taught them the necessity to act after knowing only a limited amount of information, an important principle in medical emergencies.

All the TeamSI leaders concurred that they had learned how to lead a group of participants with different levels of knowledge and understanding. They felt that they had developed the ability to grasp the essentials from a large amount of unsorted information. They had, moreover, learned to bring a group to consensus by stimulating members to discuss possible answers and find solutions among themselves. This was found to be particularly useful when handling a variety of situations when working together with people they did not know well. Furthermore, TeamSI made the leaders feel more comfortable about asking questions to resolve their own uncertainty. They believed that their TeamSI training and experiences made them less defensive and more secure. Therefore, they expressed that this helped them be safer physicians because they were more willing to question others and themselves. They further agreed that they had achieved this level of confidence as they encouraged the SI participants to do the same.

Conclusions and Lessons Learned

A well-functioning team of students, teachers, and support staff can create a highly efficient and effective learning environment at low cost to the institution (Martin and Hurley, 2005). Specifically, using SI methodology with students drawn from two different levels in a discipline can create a special type of dynamic learning environment. Both groups of students assume the role of experts in their content field, thus sharing their knowledge and stimulating one another to integrate the concepts from both areas—in this case, neurobiology and clinical neurology. These highly productive student-to-student interactions, guided by a skilled leader, deepen students' knowledge base and stimulate them to strive for content mastery.

The role of the TeamSI leader is crucial to creating this kind of learning environment. Of importance in choosing a leader is the leader's previous experience with SI, the senior status of the leader in the discipline, and the additional leadership training received. If the SI leader assumes responsibility for the group's level of interaction and productivity and if the leader has time for reflection with critical friends, she or he will grow in self-confidence and leadership skills on the team.

Both SI students and TeamSI leaders are willing to invest in the quality of the education they receive. They are highly capable of taking on responsibility for improving education for themselves and others by participating in programs and providing honest feedback about what helps and what does not. In addition, they highly value being asked to be involved in decisions that affect their education.

In the supervision sessions, as we reflected over what had taken place in the SI groups, it became obvious that there were many different reactions to the same situation. When analyzing what emotions and thoughts lay behind the reaction, we always returned to the idea that it is the SI leaders themselves who decide what choice to make and thus what the outcome will be. Therefore, we returned to the idea that we can always learn about ourselves in the encounter with others, and that there is always the possibility to choose to stay in balance, not getting frustrated but instead learning from the experience. The TeamSI leaders valued these ideas highly and were very insightful and quite generous in sharing their experiences.

Experiences from TeamSI and previous SI work have led the project director to create a leadership course for credit at Uppsala University. The course uses the SI methodology for actual performance training in leadership. Seminars devoted to creating remedies to conflict are at the heart of the curriculum. As students develop into SI leaders they become more self-aware and can see that their own attitudes and actions are reflected in the group process. The first group of students has recently completed the course with very satisfactory results. All students who have taken the course have ranked SI as very valuable.

Although SI is still a valued program and used at Uppsala University, in the Department of Neuroscience it is only running in the elective gender medicine and leadership courses. The grant from the Swedish Council for Higher Education provided generous resources for analyzing student interactions in SI, including a study of gender differences. Subsequently, the authors filmed thirty-three hours of TeamSI video and contracted for a partial analysis of the tapes. Unfortunately, the administration, which oversaw the project director's quarter-time status for the project, returned the money without written explanation to the director or notification to the University of Missouri-Kansas City. Therefore, although SI was funded for two years, only one year could be completed. The authors are committed to completing the gender study and analysis of SI interactions. These findings will be presented in a separate publication.

Both of the authors found it extremely rewarding to work with TeamSI. The students in the project were very motivated and ambitious. Attendance was excellent. This was seen as a tribute to the enthusiasm and commitment of the TeamSI leaders. The TeamSI leaders have stated that, except for the increased knowledge in neuroscience that they themselves gained by being SI leaders, they valued most of all the increased insight into and understanding of their own behavior and the leadership training. As this volume goes to press, most of the TeamSI leaders have been in practice as physicians for one to two years. When interviewed all agreed that their experience in SI had made a substantial contribution to their practice of medicine. Specifics that were mentioned included their ability to lead inclusive and productive group discussions, their ability to listen to patients and ask them meaningful questions, their ability to handle stressful and difficult situations, their heightened level of understanding and compassion for those they work with as patients and colleagues, and their ability to stay centered in an often chaotic environment.

Finally, the close collaboration on the SI team of students and staff was of deep personal significance to all involved and created lasting friendships.

References

Blanc, R. A., and Martin, D.C. "Supplemental Instruction: Increasing Student Performance and Persistence in Difficult Academic Courses." *Academic Medicine: Journal of the Association of American Medical Colleges,* 1994, 69(6), 452–454.

Costa, A., and Kallick, B. "Through the Lens of a Critical Friend." *Educational Leadership,* 1993, 51(2) 49–51.

Martin, D., and Hurley, M. "Supplemental Instruction." In H. L. Upcraft, J. N. Gardner, and B. O. Barefoot (eds.), *Challenging and Supporting the First-Year Student.* San Francisco: Jossey Bass, 2005.

Pollak, K. *No Chance Encounter: Meeting Yourself Through Others.* Findhorn, Scotland: Findhorn Press, 1998.

CARIN MUHR *is an associate professor in neurology, certified SI trainer, researcher, and senior consultant in clinical neurology at the University Hospital, Uppsala University, Uppsala, Sweden.*

DEANNA C. MARTIN *is the founder of Supplemental Instruction and founding director for the Center for Academic Development at the University of Missouri-Kansas City. Recently retired, she speaks and consults internationally on SI and its application to distance learning, VSI.*

10

SI goes beyond the traditional classroom and assists communication and education anywhere humans can be found—in industry, in cyberspace, or in the villages of the most remote corners of the world.

The New Vision for SI: Where Are We Heading?

Glen Jacobs, Marion E. Stone, M. Lisa Stout

Now in its fourth decade, Supplemental Instruction (SI) is an internationally acclaimed academic support model. Communication and critical thinking skills developed through collaborative learning are the hallmarks of the program. The learning strategies involved in the acquisition of such skills help increase academic performance and retention. The effectiveness of SI has been proven across numerous disciplines (Burmeister and others, 1994; Kenney and Kallison, 1994; Lockie and Van Lanen, 1994; Zerger, 1994) and with a variety of populations (Bidgood, 1994; Martin and Arendale, 1993; Martin, Blanc, and Arendale, 1996; Martin and Wilcox, 1996; Ramirez, 1997). In 1981, the U.S. Department of Education designated SI as a model postsecondary retention program and advocated its dissemination throughout the United States (Martin, Blanc, and DeBuhr, 1983).

Since that time, the International Center for SI has continued to train hundreds of individuals from dozens of institutions from around the world every year.

Expanding the SI Retention Model

Although SI was first launched in the early 1970s on the University of Missouri-Kansas City (UMKC) campus as a retention initiative in the School of Health Sciences (Widmar, 1994), it has, of course, expanded to a variety of other educational domains, on this campus and others. It has

NEW DIRECTIONS FOR TEACHING AND LEARNING, no. 106, Summer 2006   © Wiley Periodicals, Inc.
Published online in Wiley InterScience (www.interscience.wiley.com) • DOI: 10.1002/tl.237

been somewhat remarkable—and extremely rewarding—to see SI be so successfully implemented in such a number of different educational settings. Over the last thirty-plus years, the International Center for SI and its certified trainers around the globe have helped establish healthy SI retention programs in community colleges, liberal arts colleges, research institutions, urban-metropolitan universities, rural universities, professional schools, graduate schools, medical schools, and international schools. In addition, the SI-VSI model is currently being very successfully used in many secondary schools in the United States and abroad.

Expanding the Concept of SI

In this publication, we have begun to truly comprehend that SI is evolving beyond the traditional academic retention program that it was first designed to be. We have witnessed how the adaptation of Video-based Supplemental Instruction (VSI) has helped the vision of postsecondary education become a reality for populations that would have been previously overlooked or neglected. We have also seen how SI can be used as a tool to develop educators themselves, instilling best-teaching practices in faculty, staff, and practitioners. A very positive new outlook that has been brought to light in this volume is the identification of SI leaders as possibly among the greatest beneficiaries of the model. The skills needed to disseminate and facilitate the key ingredients of SI create well-rounded individuals who are better prepared for future careers and the current global climate.

The contributors to this volume also noted how SI can adapt to the changing structure of our higher educational system. SI is a logical partner to collaborate with innovative programs such as learning communities, teaching-learning centers, and distance learning programs.

A New Vision for SI

Supplemental Instruction's history has a solid foundation and a track record of success. With the enthusiasm and dedication of today's leadership coupled with the wisdom and forethought of the founders, the possibilities and applications for SI are boundless. There are so many directions in which SI can go. We will highlight some of these here.

SI in the Business Sector. In the near future, innovative applications of SI could be in use in the business community. The current zeitgeist of the corporate world is teamwork. The fundamental practices that are the trademark of SI lend themselves to facilitating any group of people working together. Thus, the same strategies that have been so effective in education could transfer easily into the boardroom environment. For example, SI principles could assist groups with problem solving, brainstorming, conflict resolution, or project development. Basically, communication is the key to success whether you are in the classroom or the corporate world.

In the thirty-some years since SI's inception, worldwide communication has been dramatically streamlined through the expansion of technology and advances such as computers, the World Wide Web, and a multitude of other modern conveniences. With such technological amenities, the global marketplace has an opportunity to use efficient educational tools to assist with employee training. Because many companies have satellite offices in multiple countries, or communicate with international partners, it is essential that efficient services be used to train employees and disseminate information in order to maximize workplace effectiveness. VSI might be the ideal vehicle for this venture. For example, VSI could allow employees in different countries to view the same training session while concurrently providing personalized training material and tailored facilitation. Similarly, VSI could be used to allow corporate heads in different locales to tackle difficult shared problems by jointly identifying possible solutions and developing unified plans of action. If the success of VSI in educational systems is mirrored in the business world, substantial profits are guaranteed. Through the use of the SI model and global partnerships, VSI can reap sizable financial gains for companies while simultaneously enhancing creative collaboration and improving workplace satisfaction for its employees.

Worldwide Collaborations-Expansion. Most academic support programs are either limited in their scope, unsuccessful with diverse populations, or not cost-effective; most quickly fade away. We are proud to say that SI has continued to thrive throughout its history, emerging to continually meet its intended objectives. When SI was a fledgling program at the University of Missouri-Kansas City's (UMKC) School of Dentistry (Widmar, 1994), its positive impact was instantly noted and the program soon began to grow. Through the hard work and dedication of its supporters, SI has now expanded into a worldwide educational system. Educators from fifteen hundred institutions representing twenty-nine countries have been trained by the International Center for SI and its certified SI trainers around the globe.

As an example of this global expansion, some very recent international partnerships are being implemented or strengthened. The International Center for SI has just certified SI trainers at Uppsala University in Sweden, El Universidad de Monterrey in Mexico, and the University of Wollongong in Australia. In addition, the formal partnership between the University of Missouri-Kansas City and Nelson Mandela Metropolitan University (formerly the University of Port Elizabeth) in South Africa was renewed this fall in a formal ceremony with the highest dignitaries from both institutions represented. A culmination of our efforts to convene our international colleagues will happen, as this publication goes to press, at the Fourth International Conference on SI in Malmo, Sweden. Its title: "Crossing Borders with Collaborative Learning."

Integrating SI into the Educational Systems of Developing Countries. Educational systems vary enormously around the world. Students have myriad educational and cultural backgrounds. Because of its solid basis in learning theory, active learning, and collaborative facilitation, SI's foundation can easily be modified to fit the requirements of diverse cultures, people's unique learning needs, and diverse educational systems. These systems often vary philosophically, methodologically, and in the targeted learning objectives. In many countries around the world, students are underprepared or even completely unprepared for the rigors of higher education. Students of other countries sometimes find their greatest challenges in mastering the social norms associated with a formal learning environment. Regardless of the individual's background or most salient needs, SI and its adaptations can improve and enrich his or her educational experiences.

The key delivery system that makes this possible is Video-based Supplemental Instruction (VSI), which has been noted for its use with limited resources. Dr. Deanna Martin, founder of SI, stated that VSI can "be used in any reasonable, safe and stable venue that has electricity, a VCR, a monitor, some basic supplies, and a trained facilitator" (2005, p. 8). It is rare to discover a program such as VSI that is historically successful, easily transferable to multiple populations, and yet also cost-effective and relatively easily implemented.

Historically, SI has proven itself to be a program that can be adapted to the needs of disadvantaged communities, both locally and worldwide. The efficiency and ease with which SI can be delivered is a key reason why it is so appealing for international application. SI has consistently proven to be cost-effective, highly functional with large groups, and easily adapted to diverse populations. As humankind faces overwhelming barriers to education—the primary obstacle being horrific, abject poverty—SI may be one form of relief in the battle for human betterment.

Integrating SI into Developing Countries. A particularly exciting aspect of SI is its proven ability to be a catalyst for large-scale change. Its growth in a global setting is a natural progression, because SI has already been successfully initiated in various international venues. This attribute makes SI an excellent candidate for expansion into struggling populations with a multitude of needs, especially developing countries.

SI initiates a domino effect: it benefits the targeted learners, the leaders-facilitators, the faculty-teachers, and the greater society. Furthermore, SI has the flexibility to help the wealthy as well as the impoverished, large companies as well as nonprofit agencies, urban communities as well as rural areas. In its ability to help so many institutions and populations, SI has become an institution in itself.

For example, recent headlines have documented several devastating natural disasters worldwide that have affected global education in developing countries, as well as inside the United States. By working with nonprofit agencies, such as the Red Cross, Red Crescent, and UNICEF, it is possible that the SI and VSI programs could assist in providing much-needed educational services to citizens whose lives have been disrupted and whose mass numbers are overwhelming to their communities. Many such communities are already struggling with difficulties such as poverty, lack of efficient health care, and an underfunded and inadequate educational system. Using SI to assist in such situations is among the future goals and hopes of Deanna Martin, who has stated: "I believe that we should give priority to projects that will embrace the goals of nonviolence, world peace, respect for human rights, and the education of all those who seek it" (2005, p. 10).

Conclusion

Supplemental Instruction has enjoyed thirty-some years of robust success in the world of the academy. It has proven itself to be an accomplished academic retention model, founded on a solid theoretical foundation, and supported by three decades of empirical validation. SI continues to thrive and adapt to the changing educational landscape. SI keeps in step with the times.

But SI will not be bound by the traditional confines of the university setting. Because of the model's adaptability, it can be easily modified to meet the needs of virtually any situation. We have just begun to realize the full potential SI has to offer.

References

Bidgood, P. "The Success of Supplemental Instruction: Statistical Evidence." In C. Rust and J. Wallace (eds.), *Helping Students to Learn from Each Other: Supplemental Instruction* (pp. 71–79). Birmingham, England: Staff and Educational Development Association, 1994.

Burmeister, S. L., Carter, J. M., Hockenberger, L. R., Kenney, P. A., McLaren, A., and Nice, D. "Supplemental Instruction Sessions in College Algebra and Calculus." In D. C. Martin and D. Arendale (eds.), *Supplemental Instruction: Increasing Achievement and Retention.* San Francisco: Jossey-Bass, 1994.

Kenney, P. A., and Kallison Jr., J. M. "Research Studies on the Effectiveness of Supplemental Instruction in Mathematics." In D. C. Martin and D. Arendale (eds.), *Supplemental Instruction: Increasing Achievement and Retention.* San Francisco: Jossey-Bass, 1994.

Lockie, N. M., and Van Lanen, R. J. "Supplemental Instruction for College Chemistry Courses." In D. C. Martin and D. Arendale (eds.), *Supplemental Instruction: Increasing Achievement and Retention.* San Francisco: Jossey-Bass, 1994.

Martin, D. C. "World Education Proposal." Unpublished paper, International Center for Supplemental Instruction, University of Missouri-Kansas City, 2005.

Martin, D. C., and Arendale, D. "Supplemental Instruction in the First College Year." In D. C. Martin and D. Arendale (eds.), *Supplemental Instruction: Improving First-Year Student Success in High-Risk Courses* (2nd ed., pp. 11–18). Columbia: National Resource Center for the Freshman Year Experience and Students in Transition, University of South Carolina, 1993.

Martin, D. C., Blanc, R. A., and Arendale, D. "Supplemental Instruction: Supporting the Classroom Experience. In J. N. Hankin (ed.), *The Community College: Opportunity and Access for America's First-Year Students.* Columbia: National Resource Center for the Freshman Year Experience and Students in Transition, University of South Carolina, 1996.

Martin, D. C., Blanc, R., and DeBuhr, L. "Breaking the Attrition Cycle: The Effects of Supplemental Instruction on Undergraduate Performance and Attrition." *Journal of Higher Education,* 1983, 54, 80–89.

Martin, D. C., and Wilcox, F. K. "Supplemental Instruction: Helping Students to Help Each Other." In S. Brown (series ed.) and G. Wisker (vol. ed.), *Enabling Student Learning: Systems and Strategies* (pp. 97–101). London: Kogan Page and Staff and Educational Development Association, 1996.

Ramirez, G. "Supplemental Instruction: The Long-Term Impact." *Journal of Developmental Education,* 1997, *21*(1), 2–9.

Widmar, G. E. "Supplemental Instruction: From Small Beginnings to a National Program." In D. C. Martin and D. Arendale (eds.), *Supplemental Instruction: Increasing Achievement and Retention.* San Francisco: Jossey-Bass, 1994.

Zerger, S. "Supplemental Instruction in the Content Areas: Humanities." In D. C. Martin and D. Arendale (eds.), *Supplemental Instruction: Increasing Achievement and Retention.* San Francisco: Jossey-Bass, 1994.

GLEN JACOBS *is director of and a certified SI trainer in the Center for Academic Development and the International Center for Supplemental Instruction at the University of Missouri-Kansas City.*

MARION E. STONE *is associate director and research coordinator of the Center for Academic Development and the International Center for Supplemental Instruction at the University of Missouri-Kansas City.*

M. LISA STOUT *is assistant to the director of the Center for Academic Development and the International Center for Supplemental Instruction at the University of Missouri-Kansas City.*

INDEX

Back Issue/Subscription Order Form

Copy or detach and send to:

Jossey-Bass, A Wiley Imprint, 989 Market Street, San Francisco CA 94103-1741

Call or fax toll-free: Phone 888-378-2537 6:30AM – 3PM PST; Fax 888-481-2665

Back Issues: Please send me the following issues at $29 each
(Important: please include ISBN number for each single issue you order.)

_____

_____

_____

$ _____   Total for single issues

$ _____   SHIPPING CHARGES: SURFACE   Domestic Canadian
                                      First Item $5.00 $6.00
                                      Each Add'l Item $3.00 $1.50
                   For next-day and second-day delivery rates, call the number listed above.

Subscriptions   Please __ start __ renew my subscription to _New Directions for
                 Teaching and Learning_ for the year 2__ at the following rate:

U.S.   __ Individual $80   __ Institutional $180
Canada   __ Individual $80   __ Institutional $220
All Others   __ Individual $104   __ Institutional $254
Online subscriptions available too!
**For more information about online subscriptions visit
www.interscience.wiley.com**

$ _____   Total single issues and subscriptions (Add appropriate sales tax
                   for your state for single issue orders. No sales tax for U.S.
                   subscriptions. Canadian residents, add GST for subscriptions and
                   single issues.)

__Payment enclosed (U.S. check or money order only)
__VISA __ MC __ AmEx #_____ Exp. Date _____

Signature _____ Day Phone _____
__ Bill me (U.S. institutional orders only. Purchase order required.)

Purchase order # _____
                 Federal Tax ID13559302   **GST 89102 8052**

Name _____

Address _____

_____

Phone _____ E-mail _____

For more information about Jossey-Bass, visit our Web site at **www.josseybass.com**

TL95   Problem-Based Learning in the Information Age
        Dave S. Knowlton, David C. Sharp
        Provides information about theories and practices associated with problem-
        based learning, a pedagogy that allows students to become more engaged in
        their own education by actively interpreting information. Today's professors
        are adopting problem-based learning across all disciplines to faciliate a
        broader, modern definition of what it means to learn. Authors provide
        practical experience about designing useful problems, creating conducive
        learning environments, facilitating students' activities, and assessing
        students' efforts at problem solving.
        ISBN: 0-7879-7172-3

TL94   Technology: Taking the Distance out of Learning
        Margit Misangyi Watts
        This volume addresses the possibilities and challenges of computer
        technology in higher education. The contributors examine the pressures to
        use technology, the reasons not to, the benefits of it, the feeling of being a
        learner as well as a teacher, the role of distance education, and the place of
        computers in the modern world. Rather than discussing only specific
        successes or failures, this issue addresses computers as a new cultural
        symbol and begins meaningful conversations about technology in general
        and how it affects education in particular.
        ISBN: 0-7879-6989-3

TL93   Valuing and Supporting Undergraduate Research
        Joyce Kinkead
        The authors gathered in this volume share a deep belief in the value of
        undergraduate research. Research helps students develop skills in problem
        solving, critical thinking, and communication, and undergraduate
        researchers' work can contribute to an institution's quest to further
        knowledge and help meet societal challenges. Chapters provide an overview
        of undergraduate research, explore programs at different types of
        institutions, and offer suggestions on how faculty members can find ways to
        work with undergraduate researchers.
        ISBN: 0-7879-6907-9

TL92   The Importance of Physical Space in Creating Supportive Learning
        Environments
        Nancy Van Note Chism, Deborah J. Bickford
        The lack of extensive dialogue on the importance of learning spaces in
        higher education environments prompted the essays in this volume. Chapter
        authors look at the topic of learning spaces from a variety of perspectives,
        elaborating on the relationship between physical space and learning, arguing
        for an expanded notion of the concept of learning spaces and furnishings,
        talking about the context within which decision making for learning spaces
        takes place, and discussing promising approaches to the renovation of old
        learning spaces and the construction of new ones.
        ISBN: 0-7879-6344-5

TL91   Assessment Strategies for the On-Line Class: From Theory to Practice
        Rebecca S. Anderson, John F. Bauer, Bruce W. Speck
        Addresses the kinds of questions that instructors need to ask themselves as
        they begin to move at least part of their students' work to an on-line format.
        Presents an initial overview of the need for evaluating students' on-line work
        with the same care that instructors give to the work in hard-copy format.

Helps guide instructors who are considering using on-line learning in conjunction with their regular classes, as well as those interested in going totally on-line.
ISBN: 0-7879-6343-7

TL90   Scholarship in the Postmodern Era: New Venues, New Values, New Visions
        Kenneth J. Zahorski
        A little over a decade ago, Ernest Boyer's *Scholarship Reconsidered* burst upon the academic scene, igniting a robust national conversation that maintains its vitality to this day. This volume aims at advancing that important conversation. Its first section focuses on the new settings and circumstances in which the act of scholarship is being played out; its second identifies and explores the fresh set of values currently informing today's scholarly practices; and its third looks to the future of scholarship, identifying trends, causative factors, and potentialities that promise to shape scholars and their scholarship in the new millennium.
        ISBN: 0-7879-6293-7

TL89   Applying the Science of Learning to University Teaching and Beyond
        Diane F. Halpern, Milton D. Hakel
        Seeks to build on empirically validated learning activities to enhance what and how much is learned and how well and how long it is remembered. Demonstrates that the movement for a real science of learning—the application of scientific principles to the study of learning—has taken hold both under the controlled conditions of the laboratory and in the messy real-world settings where most of us go about the business of teaching and learning.
        ISBN: 0-7879-5791-7

TL88   Fresh Approaches to the Evaluation of Teaching
        Christopher Knapper, Patricia Cranton
        Describes a number of alternative approaches, including interpretive and critical evaluation, use of teaching portfolios and teaching awards, performance indicators and learning outcomes, technology-mediated evaluation systems, and the role of teacher accreditation and teaching scholarship in instructional evaluation.
        ISBN: 0-7879-5789-5

TL87   Techniques and Strategies for Interpreting Student Evaluations
        Karron G. Lewis
        Focuses on all phases of the student rating process—from data-gathering methods to presentation of results. Topics include methods of encouraging meaningful evaluations, mid-semester feedback, uses of quality teams and focus groups, and creating questions that target individual faculty needs and interest.
        ISBN: 0-7879-5789-5

TL86   Scholarship Revisited: Perspectives on the Scholarship of Teaching
        Carolin Kreber
        Presents the outcomes of a Delphi Study conducted by an international panel of academics working in faculty evaluation scholarship and postsecondary teaching and learning. Identifies the important components of scholarship of teaching, defines its characteristics and outcomes, and explores its most pressing issues.
        ISBN: 0-7879-5447-0

NEW DIRECTIONS FOR TEACHING AND LEARNING IS NOW AVAILABLE ONLINE AT WILEY INTERSCIENCE

What is Wiley InterScience?

Wiley InterScience is the dynamic online content service from John Wiley & Sons delivering the full text of over 300 leading scientific, technical, medical, and professional journals, plus major reference works, the acclaimed Current Protocols laboratory manuals, and even the full text of select Wiley print books online.

What are some special features of Wiley InterScience?

Wiley Interscience Alerts is a service that delivers table of contents via e-mail for any journal available on Wiley InterScience as soon as a new issue is published online.

EarlyView is Wiley's exclusive service presenting individual articles online as soon as they are ready, even before the release of the compiled print issue. These articles are complete, peer-reviewed, and citable.

CrossRef is the innovative multi-publisher reference linking system enabling readers to move seamlessly from a reference in a journal article to the cited publication, typically located on a different server and published by a different publisher.

How can I access Wiley InterScience?

Visit http://www.interscience.wiley.com.

Guest Users can browse Wiley InterScience for unrestricted access to journal tables of contents and article abstracts, or use the powerful search engine.

Registered Users are provided with a *Personal Home Page* to store and manage customized alerts, searches, and links to favorite journals and articles. Additionally, Registered Users can view free online sample issues and preview selected material from major reference works.

Licensed Customers are entitled to access full-text journal articles in PDF, with select journals also offering full-text HTML.

How do I become an Authorized User?

Authorized Users are individuals authorized by a paying Customer to have access to the journals in Wiley InterScience. For example, a university that subscribes to Wiley journals is considered to be the Customer. Faculty, staff and students authorized by the university to have access to those journals in Wiley InterScience are Authorized Users. Users should contact their library for information on which Wiley journals they have access to in Wiley InterScience.

ASK YOUR INSTITUTION ABOUT WILEY INTERSCIENCE TODAY!